OS/390 MVS JCL
Quick Reference Guide
Olivia R. Carmandi

D1298524

Enjoy the book!
Olivia R. Carmandi

sponsored by:

 **Diversified Software**

For more information about our products
and services, visit our website at:
www.diversifiedsoftware.com
or call us toll free at 1-877-265-2675 or
direct at +1 (408) 778-9914

FIFTH EDITION: August 2000; Reprinted August 2003.
First Published in 1992
ISBN 1-892559-00-5

PUBLISHED BY:

MVS TRAINING, INC.

Your Complete Training Source

Airport Professional Office Center
600 Commerce Drive, Suite 605
Pittsburgh, PA 15108

Order our technical books on-line

www.mvs-training.com

To discuss your training needs or request an on-site class
call 800.356.9093 • Outside US: 412.269.9668
E-mail: sales@mvs-training.com

Printed by Schiff Printing, Pittsburgh, PA

A Tale From the Editor-in-Chief

In the quest for knowledge about methods to write efficient JCL code, a challenge was put to all people in the land who used that language: "Make the instructions clear!" At that time in the kingdom of Information Technology (IT), there was a young woman who justifiably felt overwhelmed at the volumes of information for any given topic about JCL. While perusing the many sources of information she found that they inevitably contained:

* examples that were incorrect;

* examples that were impractical; and

* examples that were not truly the best practices.

The young woman decided to take the people's challenge to produce JCL material that was accurate, concise, highly practical and contained best practice techniques. She then scribed the *MVS/JCL Quick Reference*.

Although people in the Kingdom of IT liked the idea, different publishers fought over the rights to spread the word in the kingdom. For two years, from 1992 to 1994, QED and Wiley-QED published the *MVS/JCL Quick Reference*. Finally in 1994, the young woman received official ownership of the *MVS/JCL Quick Reference* copyright and today her company, MVS Training, Inc., publishes the book.

This new edition of the book is somewhat larger in size and more than twice as long. It is easier to read, completely updated, and includes more great real-world examples, utilities, and explanations.

Technical author, David Shelby Kirk, even suggested a new name after his review of the book. He said "Survival Guide" seemed much more appropriate than Quick Reference. To paraphrase Mr. Kirk: the book is still a very manageable size and affords an enormous wealth of information.

Hope you agree. I know there's something inside the book for you as you perform your magic (work) in the kingdom of IT.

Olivia R. Carmandi

Olivia R. Carmandi, the Young Woman
Publisher and Editor-in-Chief
MVS Training, Inc.
August 2000

Special thanks to all of you for helping to make this book possible:

Sarah Weber, of MVS Training, Inc., for your editing skills, suggestions for ease of use, and continual support,

Diane Ferner, of MVS Training, Inc., for your amazing energy to get so many things done and for being an active part of the mastermind here at MVS,

Kimberly Boggs and Kay Brobeck, of MVS Training, Inc. who helped put the book together to meet our print deadline,

Bill Spires, instructor, who performed the technical review for this edition of the book,

David Shelby Kirk, noted author of numerous books for Information Technology professionals for his suggestions on organization and content,

Dr. Elena DeVos, Words At Work, for being my writing mentor since the first published article,

Lori Fabisiak, Weinrich Advertising, for her patience and attention to detail while producing the final product,

Nancy Bentley, copy editor, with a keen eye who is exceptionally good at what she does,

Bryce Taylor, of Arthur Murray, a great dance instructor who introduced a stress reducing balance in my personal life to help me meet my deadline.

Dedicated to:

My Wonderful Parents

Helen and Albert

My Beautiful Niece

Brittani Helen

Who Is A Source Of Much Inspiration To Me And To All

Those Who Have The Opportunity To Know Her

She Believes Anything Is Possible …

Table of Contents

Preface

Introduction

This book, written by my friend and colleague of the past 10 years, is intended to give you, the reader, an extensive set of practical information to help you be quickly successful in using IBM's Job Control Language (JCL) for batch processing. I'm aware of no other book that has this goal.

Focus

The focus of the book is on developing your survival skills quickly, helping you grasp and understand major concepts and terms so you can be productive in days; not weeks or months. JCL is an intense and complex computing skill and highly-valued in the industry. Traditionally, learning JCL takes years, learning small components at a time. Many programmers and operators even tually give up the chase. This book will help ensure that you don't.

Format

Unlike a traditional textbook on JCL, this book covers the foundation material quickly and then proceeds to demonstrate with examples so you can easily convert the concept into real work situations. Once you've read the initial material, you can quickly jump from section to section.

Audience

This book is for people in programming and operations areas, working in a mainframe OS/390 MVS environment. The version of MVS being used (e.g., MVS/XA, MVS/ESA, OS/390) does not matter for purposes of this book. Where new features are explicit to a particular version that is identified in the book.

Reading Recommendation

For the quickest benefit, skim through the book quickly, noting new words and concepts. Then, in your work environment, turn to the appropriate sections as you face new JCL challenges.
The examples will help you succeed.

Conclusion

To paraphrase the line, "this is not your father's JCL manual." This book is not a thousand pages of prose, explaining every conceivable element that might appear in JCL. Instead, it focuses on what is actually being used in the computing world and packages it for easy consumption. I wish such a book had been available when I was learning JCL many years ago.

Happy Reading!!!

David Shelby Kirk, August, 2000

Command Syntax

- Brackets [ ] indicates parameters in brackets are optional. Do not key the brackets as part of the statement.

- | indicates choose one of the operands do not key the |.

Best Practice techniques

This quick reference lists a preferred method of coding JCL throughout.

- Most workable—For instance, parentheses are not always needed around the accounting field yet the accounting field is always shown with the parentheses.

- Suggestions to promote more efficient JCL code— For example, passing temporary data sets to another step is discouraged.

- Suggestions to make code uniform and easier to maintain—For instance, user should always code all 3 subparameters of DISP so there is no guessing as to what the default is.

- This quick reference contains the statements and parameters that are most often used and the best way to use them.

Consistent JCL Code and JCL Standards

- Please be consistent when creating JCL and do not adopt bad coding habits because they propagate throughout the shop.

- When you read "See standards" this means your shop's JCL standards.

- Use the shop's JCL standards. If the standards are not clear or lacking information, then follow the procedures to update them!

Standards and procedures allow users to adapt more readily to technological change. When your shop develops and follows standards and procedures this helps you to:

- Adapt more easily to technological change.

- Be more productive in less time.

- Train new people consistently and easily.

- Produce timely and accurate work results, and improve morale.

Introduction to JCL 1

JCL is the IBM mainframe Job Control Language, a sequence of statements identifying a unit of *batch work* (a job) to the operating system OS/390 MVS.*

Batch work runs in the background; depending upon the complexity of the program and the amount of data, a job may run for hours. Many jobs can run at once. Sometimes jobs access the same data or have higher priorities. These items are handled using automated scheduling software.

With *online work*, requests or commands are performed immediately in the foreground. Take the Internet, for instance: when the system is performing a search the user has to wait until it responds before the system can perform another task. One of the ways OS/390 allows online access to users is through Time Sharing Option (TSO), where users can create and update JCL.

JCL communicates to the system the "Who", "What", "When", "Where", and "How" of a given job run.

The Who:

JCL assigns a job name and details the specific characteristics of a job run such as charge back information and brief description of the job run.

In the job statement (See Figure 1.) the job name is listed in columns 3-10, accounting detail is listed within parentheses in columns 17-25, and a description of the job is listed within apostrophes in columns 29-39.

---

*   OS is Operating System, MVS stands for Multiple Virtual Storage—IBM's earlier name for their OS/390 operating system. For more information on OS/390 MVS read "MVS for OS/390 Primer" in-depth book #2 from the MVS Training, Inc. Mainframe Series by David Shelby Kirk.

The What:

JCL signals the program(s) to run or execute. JCL triggers the use of Input and Output (I/O) files or data sets, as the program(s) require.

In the Sample JCL (See Figure 1.) the EXEC PGM line 5 provides the program name. Lines 6-10 list Data Definitions (DDs) or I/O data sets.

The When:

JCL indicates the frequency of a production job run. Using good JCL standards, "D" denotes daily, W means weekly and so on. (See Figure 1.) These indicators can be found within the job name in columns 3-10 of statement #1.

The job runs when the user SUBmits (SUB) the job through "TSO/ISPF" or via an automated job scheduling software tool such as IBM's "OPC" or Computer Associates' "CA-7".

The Where:

JCL determines where the job will run and directs the job's output.

(See Figure 1.) CLASS parameter provides initiator where job will run. MSGCLASS parameter directs where JCL statements and messages will print.

The How:

JCL can specify the upper limit of storage needed by the program(s).

(See Figure 1.) REGION parameter gives a maximum amount of storage to run the job.

Columns

```
     1               1   11                2
                     2   67                9

 1. //PAW010    JOB (acct-info),'description',
 2. //              CLASS=x,
 3. //              MSGCLASS=x,
 4. //              REGION=#
 5. //GEN010    EXEC PGM=IEBGENER
 6. //SYSIN     DD   DUMMY
 7. //SYSUT1    DD   DSN=input.data.set,
 8. //              DISP=SHR
 9. //SYSUT2    DD   SYSOUT=x
10. //SYSPRINT  DD   SYSOUT=x
11. //
```

Figure 1 Sample JCL

- In Figure 1 line numbers on left are added for readability. Column numbers are shown across top for readability and JCL is a column sensitive language.

1.1. JCL SOFTWARE PRODUCTS

Skilled application of JCL demands a working knowledge of the components: the way in which these elements command a sophisticated operating system enables the user to take fullest advantage of available options.

Managing information requires a user to juggle a vast array of tasks and tools. One needs to master the optimal organization and technique of JCL coding. Efficient formatting of commands and statements and consistent structuring of the language is a must. It is also essential to be at ease with JCL compatible software. A range of programs from maintenance to mainframe/time-sharing access software richly enhance the user's experience with JCL.

Software products specifically designed to enhance JCL have an impressive range of features and applications. In a corporate environment these products are highly sought after, as they maximize the efficiency of tasks performed, ultimately saving time and money. For the user, these products simply make life with JCL much easier. Here are two such software products.

1.1.1. PRO/JCL or JOB/SCAN from Diversified Software Systems, Inc.

This software enhances the quality of JCL, making it more user friendly and more manageable. As a result, JCL related application outages are eliminated. *Diversified Software Systems, Inc.* developed JOB/SCAN and later the newer version, PRO/JCL to help achieve a high quality production environment, increase staff output, and save money on a long-term basis.

SOFTWARE BENEFITS:

* Reformats and standardizes JCL to be user friendly (See "Consistent and Structured JCL" found later in chapter).

* Helps you complete production changes and conversions in a more timely manner.

* Catches major JCL errors before job is submitted to run, helping to eliminate production application failures—especially useful in a production environment.

* Enables users to automatically implement JCL standards via the REXX language (IBM's scripting language) for PRO/JCL, or via COBOL, for their JOB/SCAN software product; this promotes coding consistency that's easily maintained and updated.

For more information visit ***www.diversifiedsoftware.com***

1.1.2. MVS/Quick-Ref from Chicago-Soft, Ltd.

This tool allows easy on-line access to syntax and messages; it also stores company documentation for OS/390 MVS users.
It provides a means of increasing the breadth of the use of JCL by allowing a user to do more with the language and errors by easily accessing the information on-line.

SOFTWARE BENEFITS:

- Contains IBM and third party error messages. Users simply place the cursor on the message and hit the PF key to display information regarding the error.

- Furnishes the syntax for JCL, IDCAMS, COBOL, REXX, utilities, operator commands, and so on, via an easy-to-use format.

- Expands the product's usefulness by including a glossary of terms such as HTML, UNIX, etc.

- Equips the user with a database facility so that shops can create and store their own unique information on-line.

- Provides off-site technical support without establishing a connection to the mainframe, while still keeping the quality/quantity of information.

- Can be used "over top of" ISPF—the friendly interface to IBM's Time Sharing Option for the mainframe; MVS/Quick-Ref is the "hit and run" information access software.

For more information visit *www.chicago-soft.com*

1.2. TYPES OF DATA SETS & THEIR ORGANIZATION

* In OS/390 data records are stored as FILES, often referred to as DATA SETS. These terms are interchangeable. To store and easily retrieve information entered into a data set, there must be an order or process by which this can be achieved.

* Data Organization is the method used to organize, store, and retrieve records in a data set. Data set organizations are: Sequential, VSAM, Partitioned, Direct Access, and PDSE. They are presented in the order in which they are used within or with JCL.

1.2.1. Sequential Data Sets

* A sequential data set processes records in the order in which they were written. Organization is Physical Sequential (PS). Data sets can be sorted to rearrange their order. Often they contain input to programs or are output from programs. These data sets are typically created using JCL during the job run. Types of physical sequential data sets follow.

  * Simple data set—consists of a data set with a unique name. Example:

    PAYP.SIMPLE

  * Generation Data Group (GDG)—consists of up to 255 versions of the data set with the same data set name but containing different data. (System appends a G000#V00 to the data set name.) Example:

PAYP.GDG.MAST(-1)	OLDER	PAYP.GDG.MAST.G0005V00
PAYP.GDG.MAST(+0)	CURRENT	PAYP.GDG.MAST.G0006V00
PAYP.GDG.MAST(+1)	CREATE	PAYP.GDG.MAST.G0007V00

- Temporary data set—exists only during the run of the job. Therefore restart must occur in the step that created the temporary data set so a step or steps that ran successfully must be rerun due to the use of the temporary data set. A temporary data set has a specific symbol structure. There are 2 "&" characters preceding the temporary data set name. Example:

  &&TEMP

☞ Suggest user avoid this poor coding technique, as system cannot step restart the job.

✐ *See: Data Set Name.*

Data Record #1
Data Record #2
Data Record #3
...
Data Record n

Physical Sequential

1.2.2. VSAM Data Set

- VSAM is an access method for direct or sequential processing of either fixed or variable-length records on direct access devices.

- Virtual storage involves the use of aspects of virtual memory; this type of memory management allows a program to address memory from a logical point of view without regard to the amount of memory that's physically available. While the program is run, only a portion of the program/data is kept in real memory. This way the user can access a memory space larger than that of real memory. Records in a VSAM data set are organized using these unique facets of virtual storage and give the user a broad range of approaches to data set/file access and storage. VSAM data set records can be organized in four ways:

  1) Entry Sequenced Data (ESDS) acts like a physical sequential data set.

  2) Key Sequenced Data Set (KSDS) is processed sequentially either in order or randomly by key field.

  3) Linear Data Set (LDS) processes using IBM's Data Windowing Services (DWS) and is compatible with high-level languages such as (COBOL); it is not often used.

  4) Relative Record Data Set acts as a direct data set.

- KSDS is the most commonly used VSAM organizational method for records. KSDS contains a key field that uniquely identifies a record. These data sets contain input to programs and can be updated by programs. (VS displays when user views data set information on-line using TSO/ISPF screen 3.2.)

- VSAM data sets are typically created and loaded in a separate job using the IBM utility *IDCAMS*—also known as *access method services*. IDCAMS allows the user to create and maintain the Virtual Storage Access Method. With IDCAMS the user deletes, defines, and copies information into the data set. Records are physically stored in a *Data Area* in order by contents of key field. A separate copy of the key fields is stored in order inside the *Index Area.*

  ⟨✎⟩ *See: IDCAMS DEFINE VSAM.*

Index Area points to data records

    A = Records 1 to 10

    B = Records 11 to 20 . . .

Data Area contains data records

    Data Record 1   Key = A

    . . .

    Data Record 10 Key = A

    Data Record 11 Key = B ...

VSAM KSDS

1.2.3. Partitioned Data Set (PDS)

- A PDS stores related records in partitions or (members) of one large data set rather than separately as many small data sets. A PDS is also called a library.

- Organization is Partitioned Organization (PO). Libraries contain a specific type of related members, similar to your local library where a shelf of related books would be the PDS and a specific book would be the member. Members are representations of data; each member has a unique name and contains one or more records. Records are written and retrieved sequentially. Examples of members from JCL libraries follow:

- JCL found in a library such as PROD.JCLLIB contains these types of JCL statements:

```
//jobname   JOB (acct),'pgm-name',
//          CLASS=x,
//          MSGCLASS=x
//JOBLIB    DD  DSN=library,
//          DISP=SHR
//          JCLLIB ORDER=(library1,library2)
//jobstep   EXEC PROC=procname
//
```

- The above statements direct the system to identify the job name and job libraries used, and define the procedure to be executed.

- PROCs found in a library such as PROD.PROCLIB contains these types of JCL statements:

```
//procname PROC
//*                       comments
//procstep EXEC PGM=pgmname
//ddname    DD  DSN=dataset.name,
//          DISP=…
//ddname    DD  SYSOUT=x
//SYSIN     DD  DSN=PROD.PARMLIB(member),
//          DISP=SHR
```

- The above statements are included in a PROC and direct the system to identify the programs to execute. The Data Definition (DD) statements indicate the input and output data sets used by the programs.

- Control Statements found in a library such as PROD.PARMLIB contains these types of statements. Notice that these statements do not contain a // or /* in columns 1 and 2:

  ```
  SORT FIELDS=(1,20,A),FORMAT=CH
  ```

- The above statement is a command to the program and statement format varies per program.

- Program libraries contain:

  1) Source Programs

  2) Load Modules

- A source program is the code written by an application programmer. A load module is an executable unit compiled and possibly linked with other programs.

Directory-points to members
Pointer to Member #1
Pointer to Member #2 ...
Pointer to Member #n
Member 1—Data Record
Data Record #2
Data Record #3
Member 2—Data Record
Data Record #2
Data Record #3
Member 3—Data Record
Data Record #2
Data Record #3
Member #n ...

Partitioned Data Set, also called a Library

1.2.4. Direct Access Data Set

*   Direct Access stores records physically in the order in which they were written. Direct data sets are processed randomly using a record number. Data set organization is Direct Access (DA).

*   Examples of products that manage libraries using direct access are CA-Panvalet, CA-Librarian. Due to the direct access organization, to view or edit library members on-line the user must go to a different set of ISPF panels supplied by the vendor.

```
Data Record  #1
Data Record  #2
Data Record  #3
Data Record  #n ...
```

Direct Access

1.2.5. Partitioned Data Set Extended (PDSE)*

A PDSE provides a new type of partitioned data set available with IBM's Storage Management System (SMS). Organization is partitioned organization but the type is a LIBRARY, as opposed to a PDS. Main IBM products to support SMS are:

*   Data Facility Hierarchical Storage Manager (DF/HSM)—handles when data sets should be migrated to tape based upon last time accessed (brains).

*   Data Facility Data Set Services (DF/DSS)—moves data sets (workhorse). Can be used to quickly back up and restore application data sets or entire volumes.

*   A PDSE is structured and functions the same as a PDS but has advantages:

    *   Directory expands as members are added; the size is not fixed.

    *   Directory searches are faster.

    *   Space gets dynamically reused; there is no need to compress PDSEs.

---

* *PDSEs are meant for large libraries and are usually allocated by the system's personnel not by individual users. SMS must be active to allocate a PDSE.*

1.3. JCL STATEMENT FORMAT

Information Technology has developed into a community of cooperating systems that allow the users of our world to interface with it, with one another, and with information of a mind-boggling degree of variety and complexity. The interaction requires highly organized languages. There are languages to assist in the operations of every kind of system. One of several such languages is JCL, a sequence of commands to identify a job to a particular operating system as well as to describe the characteristics of that job. JCL promotes communication between the user and the operating system and in reverse. The language's constructs are paramount to knowing and fully using the system. The following sections illustrate the workings of these linguistic components.

1.3.1. Statement Components

A JCL statement is used to identify the job, define it, and describe its requirements to the operating system. Here is how a JCL statement is constructed.

Columns

```
  123        1   1                              77      8
             2   6                              23      0
  _____
  //name     oper  parameter optional comment       ignored
  //               parameter=(subparameter,…)
```

- // or /* is found in columns 1 and 2. Sometimes there are non-JCL statements intermixed in the job run; this identifies a JCL statement to the system.

- Name—Specifies statement name. Code in columns 3 to 10 up to 8 alphanumeric or national characters. First character MUST be alphabetic or national—#, $, @.

- Oper—Operation—Identifies the statement type. System requires at least 1 space before and after operation. For consistency start coding in column 12. Some common operations are: JOB, EXEC, DD, OUTPUT, and PROC.

- Parameter—Specifies detail about the statement type. Parameters are made up of subparameters. There are 2 types of parameters and subparameters. They are positional and keyword:

1) *POSITIONAL*—There are 2 types of positional. They are *positional parameters* and *positional subparameters.*

   a) *Positional parameters* precede keyword parameters. Examples below are accounting and programmer name parameters.

   b) Parameters can consist of *positional subparameters*; while the parameters are not positional, the subparameters are.

- *Positional subparameters* must be coded in order e.g., (subparameter1, subparameter2, subparameter3).

- When omitting a subparameter, a comma must be coded. The system uses system defaults, e.g., (,,subparameter3).

- When subparameter is last, don't code the comma e.g., (subparameter,subparameter2).

Positional Parameter Example

```
//name     JOB (acct-info),'prog-name'…
```

- Acct-info and the prog-name parameters are usually positional (shop specific).

- These must be coded per shop's standards after JOB in the order shown.

Positional Subparameter Example

```
//                    DISP=(NEW,CATLG,DELETE)
```

- DISP is a keyword parameter. Keyword parameters may have positional subparameters.

- (NEW,CATLG,DELETE) are positional subparameters. If NEW is not coded, the comma must be coded, e.g., (,CATLG,DELETE).

☞ Suggest coding all 3 subparameters to avoid confusion.

2) *KEYWORD*

a) Keyword parameters can be coded in any order.

b) Examples are CLASS, MSGCLASS, and REGION. See Figure 1.

- Comment—Provides great internal documentation on a statement.

- Leave at least 1 space to code a comment on a statement.

- If coding goes beyond column 71 on the last parameter of a statement, a JCL error appears that is hard to detect because column 72 is a continuation column.

Comment on a JCL Statement Example

```
                                                    7
                                                    2
//DDIN      DD   DSN=ABCP.SIMPLE
//               DISP=SHR              COMMENT
```

- Continuation—Column 72 is a continuation column. The continuation column should always be blank.

- Not Used—Columns 73-80 are not used. System can write sequence numbers in these columns.

1.3.2. Statement Names

JCL statements can contain names in columns 3-10. On some statements name is optional but should still be coded. Below are rules and guidelines to successfully code statement names.

Statement names are 1 to 8 alphanumeric characters. The first character must be alphabetic or national—@, #, $. Statement names include:

- Jobname—occurs on JOB statement. Test job names often consist of the person's logon ID, plus at least one character. Production job name requirements are specified in the shop's JCL standards.
  See Figure 1 for an example.

- Jobstepname—occurs on EXEC PROC or EXEC statement.

- Procname—occurs on PROC statement.

- Stepname—occurs on EXEC PGM in "Plain JCL". Plain JCL is JCL that is not in PROC format.

    See: *Three Ways to Code JCL.*

- Procstepname—occurs on EXEC PGM in a PROC.

- DDname—occurs on DD statements. DD name should indicate data set usage (e.g., last character, I—Input, O—Output, U—Update, R—Report).

    ☞ Suggest always coding name on above statements.

- Name—occurs on other JCL statements. For instance, name is required on the OUTPUT statement because a SYSOUT statement uses name to point back to OUTPUT statement.

- For IF/THEN/ELSE/ENDIF, INCLUDE, JCLLIB, and SET, name is optional.

    ☞ Suggest not coding name on these statements.

1.3.3. Data Set Names

- Data Set Name is assigned to a collection of related data records. Data set name occurs after the DD DSN= ... keyword. Data set name is comprised of multiple nodes that contain from 1 to 8 characters. Each node is separated by a period. (An Example is: PROD.DATA.SET) The first node is often called the high-level qualifier; second node is the second-level qualifier, and so on. Each qualifier must begin with an alphabetic or national character (e.g., $, @, #). Name can be up to 44 characters, including the periods up to 35 characters for a generation data set (GDS).

```
//SIMPLEOT DD   DSN=PROD.DATA.SET,
//               DISP=(NEW,CATLG,DELETE),
// ...
//GDGOT    DD   DSN=PROD.GDG.DATASET(+1),
//               DISP=(NEW,CATLG,DELETE),
// ...
```

- Temporary data set begins with two ampersands followed by a 1 to 8 character name and is deleted by the system when the job ends.

- Temporary data set example shows PASS to send the data set to another step within the same job. Avoid because this does not allow step restart:

```
//TEMPOT   DD   DSN=&&TEMP,
//               DISP=(NEW,PASS,DELETE),
//...
```

1.3.4. Physical Sequential Data Set Usage Guidelines

* As mentioned earlier the 3 types of physical sequential data sets are: simple, temporary, and Generation Data Group (GDG).

* Simple data set means that the data set was created in a job, used in another step in the same job, but not used in other jobs. This is the author's meaning but many shops use these data sets in other jobs. When a simple data set is going to be used by other jobs, her preference is to make that data set a GDG, even if only 1 generation is kept. This can be a method to indicate that the data set is accessed by other jobs, so do not delete the data set at job end.

* For simple data sets accessed in only one job, efficient JCL standards insist that the data set be given a qualified name and be cataloged instead of using a temporary data set to allow step restart:

```
//DDOUT     DD  DSN=PAYP.SIMPLE.SORTED,
//              DISP=(NEW,CATLG,DELETE)...
```

☞ Suggest promoting job step restart by allowing only temporary data set usage when data set is created and used in the same step. Then you do not need to give the data set a name, e.g., sort work files.

```
//SORTWK01 DD  UNIT=SYSDA,
//              SPACE=(CYL,(50,5))
```

* The last time the simple data set is used, code JCL to allow job step restart. Don't waste computer resources rerunning steps because JCL was coded inadequately. Here's an example: OLD means data set exists, DELETE says delete and uncatalog the data set if step completes normally, KEEP means KEEP the data set if step abends so user can restart at that step:

```
//DDIN      DD  DSN=PAYP.SIMPLE.SORTED,   *LAST USE
//              DISP=(OLD,DELETE,KEEP)
```

* Simple data set accessed by other jobs:

```
//DDIN      DD  DSN=PAYP.SIMPLE.SORTED,   *LAST USE
//              DISP=(OLD,KEEP,KEEP)
```

* Use a GDG to keep multiple versions for recovery and as stated above if data set is accessed by other jobs.

1.4. CONSISTENT AND STRUCTURED JCL

JCL structuring guidelines help make JCL easier to read, modify, and use.

- Code one parameter per line.

  ✐ See: *Examples throughout reference.*

- Use consistent indentation (e.g., JOB, EXEC, DD begin in column 12; continuation lines begin in column 16).

- Place input statements before output.

- Code: keyword parameters in the same sequence (e.g., DSN then DISP).

- Use meaningful names (e.g., UPDAT05, REPT10, SORT20 for step name). PROC and JCL member names should be derived from job name.

- Specify parameters at one level only.

  ✐ See: *COND, REGION, TIME.*

- Use comments before steps. They are internal documentation that facilitates job restart.

- Do not code unnecessary JCL statements or parameters.

1.5. STATEMENT CONTINUATIONS

• Continuation allows user to code 1 parameter per line, resulting in JCL that's easier to update and use. The line before the continuation must end in a comma. Actual continuation parameter cannot start beyond column 16. Last parameter of the statement contains no comma at the end.

• Do not code characters in column 72, as this also indicates a continuation. If a continuation parameter is coded beyond column 16, the following JCL error will appear:

"EXPECTED CONTINUATION NOT FOUND"

Continuation Format

```
1              1   1                                    7
               2   6                                    2
//ddname    DD   DSN=data.set.name,
//               parameter,      *CONTINUATION ,
//               parameter       *LAST HAS NO ,
```

• Numbers 1, 12, 16... depict column numbers. Continuation parameter cannot start beyond column 16. Previous line ends in a comma; last line has no comma, as the JCL comments state.

Continuation Example

```
//SYSIN    DD   DSN=PROD.PARMLIB(MEMA),
//               DISP=(SHR,KEEP,KEEP)
```

• Shows a comma at end of first line, last line has no comma. Comments are not coded in this example.

Major Statements Including ESA   **2**

This chapter covers the major statements needed to create JCL to run a batch job. Statements are listed in alphabetic order and include the following.

Comment—Supplies user-friendly documentation.

DD—Lists the data sets being read and created during job execution.

- This includes the SYSIN DD where control statements are read as input.

- Also includes the SYSOUT parameter where printed output is directed.

DD DUMMY parameter (or NULLFILE)—Means that the DD is ignored for this job run.

EXEC PGM—Gives the load module to execute along with the older technique to check return codes to determine if step execution should occur.

EXEC PROC—Calls a cataloged procedure to run. The cataloged procedure can contain multiple EXEC PGMs.

IF/THEN/ELSE/ENDIF—Gives an additional newer, easier to understand method for checking return codes. This book lists how the new IF statements differ from the old COND parameter.

JCLLIB—Gives an improved way to tell the system where to find the cataloged procedure and any INCLUDE members.

JOB—Identifies the unit of batch work to the system.

JOBLIB—Lists the libraries where the system searches for the application load modules for the entire job.

NULL—Indicates end of job JCL.

OUTPUT—Extends the options for printed output.

PROC—Indicates beginning of a cataloged procedure.

SET—Allows use of symbolics in plain JCL.

STEPLIB—Gives an alternative to JOBLIB but must be coded at each step level. This means user must add a STEPLIB for each EXEC PGM.

2.1. COMMENT STATEMENT

- A comment statement provides internal documentation, an addendum or supplement to the code to further define its purpose or meaning. Comments can be coded anywhere in the JCL, except before the JOB statement. Columns 1-3 contain //*, then any characters in columns 4-72.

- Comments can also be coded as part of the statement by leaving at least one blank, then coding up to column 71.

- Comments do not appear on the master console as they did in the DOS/VSE operating system.

  ☞ Suggest using comments—also called a flower box—as shown below before each job step (EXEC PGM statement).

Comment Format

```
//* ANY CHARACTERS UP TO COL 72
```

Comment Examples

```
//**********************************************
//* WHAT   STEP  DOES - UPDATES VSAM   FILE
//* GIVE   RESTART   INSTRUCTIONS
//**********************************************
```

Comment on a Statement Format

```
//ddname   DD  parameter,     comment
//               parameter     comment
```

Comment on a Statement Example

```
//FILEIN   DD  DSN=PAYP.DATA,     INPUT
//               DISP=(SHR,KEEP,KEEP)
```

- Remember leave at least 1 blank to code a comment on a statement.

2.2. DD STATEMENT

- Data Definition (DDs) statements describe input and output files or data sets accessed by the program. DDs are coded after the EXEC PGM statement. User must specify all DDs opened by the program. This means user must code a DD for each data set program accesses. Following are the most commonly coded DD parameters.

  ↳ **See:** *When to Code DD Parameters for additional DD parameters.*

☞ **Caution:** There is a maximum of approximately 3,000 DDs per step. (This varies per shop). A colleague and fellow author Gabe Gargiulo recently e-mailed me to share that he witnessed a job that had too many DD statements. He wrote:

> "JES2 ABEND!
>
> A job with over 1000 DD * statements brought JES2 to its knees, stopping all initiators, started tasks, sub systems, IMS batch and message regions, TSO logons, and the Coke machine. After I submitted this job, all activity stopped on 2 CPU's—the production one, and the test one!
>
> IBM said upgrade Jes2!
>
> Company said "we will!"
>
> Moral—don't overdo the DD * statements in a job!
>
> OK, I made up the part about the Coke machine."
> gabe

- Ddname—ties the DD statement to the program and is coded in columns 3–10 of DD statement.

  ↳ **See:** *Statement Names, ddname.*

DD Format

```
//ddname    DD   DSN=data.set.name,
//               DISP=(begin,normal-step,abend-step),
//               UNIT=unitname,
//               VOL=SER=nnnnnn,
//               SPACE=(type,(primary,secondary),RLSE),
//               DCB=(model.dscb,RECFM=x,LRECL=#,BLKSIZE=##)
```

COBOL Program Example

```
PROGRAM-ID.  PAYUPDT.
ENVIRONMENT DIVISION.
CONFIGURATION SECTION.
INPUT-OUTPUT SECTION.
FILE-CONTROL.
      SELECT  TRANS-IN    ASSIGN  TO  PAYI.
      SELECT  RPT-OUT     ASSIGN  TO  CHECKO.
      SELECT  MASTER      ASSIGN  TO  MASTU...
```

• SELECT...ASSIGN—lists the DD names that will be needed to run the program.

Plain JCL Example to Run COBOL Program

```
//TBRITT2  JOB (BIL,1234),'BRITTANI 2222',
//            CLASS=A,
//            MSGCLASS=X,
//            NOTIFY=TBRITT
//JOBLIB   DD  DSN=TEST.LOADLIB,
//            DISP=SHR
//* * * * * * * * * * * * * * * * * * * *
//PS010    EXEC PGM=PAYUPDT
//PAYI     DD  DSN=PAYP.DATA.IN,
//            DISP=SHR
//MASTU    DD  DSN=PAYP.VSM.MASTER,
//            DISP=SHR
//CHECKO   DD  SYSOUT=S
//SYSOUT   DD  SYSOUT=*
//SYSUDUMP DD  SYSOUT=*
//
```

• DD names PAYI, CHECKO, MASTU must be included in the JCL.

2.2.1. DD Format—DSN

`//ddname   DD   DSN=data.set.name,`

DD Parameters—DSN

- DSN—supplies a 44-character identifier for the data set.

  ↪ *See: Data Set Names.*

2.2.2. DD Format—DISP

`//                DISP=(begin,normal,abend)`

DD Parameters—DISP

- DISP—Gives status of data set, what to do with data set if step ends normally, what to do with data set if step blows up.

  - *Begin* value gives status of the data set when the step starts.

  - *Normal-step* value tells the system what to do when step completes successfully.

  - *Abend-step* value tells the system what to do when step blows up. Contains positional subparameters:

  `//                DISP=(begin;normal,abend)`

☞ CAUTION: Blow up or ABEND means job receives an error and system stops processing. If job receives an invalid return code from a utility like SORT, job will continue to run unless user codes JCL to halt the run. Also, with an invalid return code the *normal-step* DISP value is used.

  ↪ *See: COND and IF...ENDIF.*

☞ CAUTION: When DISP is not coded the default is:

`//                DISP=(NEW,DELETE,DELETE)`

- *Begin values are:*

  NEW   — Creates a data set.

  OLD   — Gives exclusive use to existing data set.

  SHR   — Allows multiple users to access existing data set.

  MOD   — Gives exclusive use and either adds records to end of existing data set or creates a data set.

- *Normal and abend values can be:*

  CATLG   — Saves data set and enters in catalog. When coded with NEW creates a cataloged output data set.

  DELETE   — Deletes and uncatalogs data set.

  UNCATLG— Removes catalog entry.

  KEEP   — If data set exists retains, a non-temporary data set. For tape data sets the tape is rewound and dismounted.

               If data set does not exist, creates and retains, but does not catalog when coded with NEW except with SMS.

         See: *SMS Rules.*

         Suggest user not code for output data sets NEW, and KEEP, i.e., NEW,KEEP,KEEP or NEW,CATLG,KEEP

  PASS   — Passes to another job step. Saves time because system doesn't have to look up the data set location and volume. Tape repositions to beginning and stays mounted.

         Suggest user always code all 3 subparameters. Shop might make an exception for SHR. The 3 subparameter rule should be in shop's standards.

DISP—Cataloged Input Examples

DISP—VSAM Share—Example 1

```
//VSAMI    DD   DSN=ABCP.VMSTR,        *VSAM
//               DISP=(SHR,KEEP,KEEP)
   or
//               DISP=SHR
```

- DISP=SHR is coded 99% of the time when accessing VSAM data sets, as access is controlled when the data set is defined using IDCAMS utility.

- When SHR is coded the default is SHR,KEEP,KEEP.

- *VSAM is a comment.

  See: When to Code DD Parameters, DISP.

DISP—GDG—Exclusive Use—Example 2

```
//MSTRI    DD   DSN=ABCP.GMSTR(+0),      *UPDATE GDG
//               DISP=(OLD,KEEP,KEEP)
   or
//               DISP=OLD
```

- OLD gives exclusive use; no one else can access the data set. Use to read current generation +0 and create a new generation.

- When OLD is coded the default is OLD,KEEP,KEEP.

- *UPDATE GDG—is a comment.

DISP—Simple Data Set Going to Another Job—Example 3

```
//SIMPI    DD   DSN=ABCP.SIMPLE,
//               DISP=(SHR,KEEP,KEEP)
```

- SHR allows access to other users.

DISP—Simple Not Going to Another Job—Example 4

```
//SIMPIN   DD   DSN=ABCP.SIMPLE,         *LAST USE
//               DISP=(OLD,DELETE,KEEP)
```

- OLD gives exclusive use, DELETE if step completes normally, KEEP if step abends, so user can step restart the job.

DISP—Not Cataloged Input—Tape from Outside

```
//MSTRI    DD  DSN=XYZ.DATA,
//              DISP=(OLD,KEEP,KEEP),
//              UNIT=CART,          *NEED UNIT
//              VOL=SER=123456      *NEED VOLSER
```

• Data set is coming from outside the company. Therefore the data set is not cataloged to the user's system, so UNIT and VOL=SER are required to read the data set.

&✐ *See: EXPDT=98000.*

DISP—Cataloged Output Examples

DISP—Cataloged GDG Output—Example 1

```
//MSTRO    DD  DSN=ABCP.GMSTR(+1),
//              DISP=(NEW,CATLG,DELETE), ...
```

DISP—Cataloged Simple Output—Example 2

```
//MSTRO    DD  DSN=ABCP.SIMPLE,
//              DISP=(NEW,CATLG,DELETE), ...
```

DISP—PASS Output—Example 3

☞ Suggest avoiding this poor coding technique, as this does not allow step restart. Give the data set a qualified name as shown in the Simple Example above and catalog the data set when creating it to allow step restart.

```
//DDOT     DD  DSN=&&TEMP,
//              DISP=(NEW,PASS,DELETE), ...
```

2.2.3. DD Format—UNIT

```
//ddname    DD  DSN=data.set.name,
//              DISP=(begin,normal-step,abend-step),
//              UNIT=unitname, …
```

DD Parameter—UNIT

* UNIT—Specifies where to write the data set. UNIT might not be needed when writing to DASD in an SMS environment.

* Also indicates where to find the data set when accessing a data set that is not cataloged, such as a tape from outside the company.

   ☞ **See:** *Not Cataloged Input Example above.*

UNIT Write to DASD—Example 1

```
//MSTRO     DD  DSN=ABCP.GMSTR(+1),
//              DISP=(NEW,CATLG,DELETE),
//              UNIT=SYSDA, …              DASD
```

UNIT Write to Tape—Example 2

```
//MSTRO     DD  DSN=ABCP.GMSTR(+1),
//              DISP=(NEW,CATLG,DELETE),
//              UNIT=CART,      …          TAPE
```

2.2.4. DD Format—VOL=SER

```
//ddname    DD  DSN=data.set.name,
//              DISP=(begin,normal-step,abend-step),
//              VOL=SER=volser
```

DD Parameter—VOL=SER

• VOL=SER—Specifies a specific volume indicating where to write the data set. When coded on output data sets in an SMS environment the VOL=SER parameter is usually ignored. The system chooses the appropriate volume.

• Also specifies where to find the data set when accessing a data set that is not cataloged, such as a tape from outside the company.

☞ **See:** *Not Cataloged Input Example above.*

VOL=SER Write to DASD—Example (Older Coding Technique)

☞ Suggest avoiding this poor coding technique; let the system choose the volume.

```
//MSTRO     DD  DSN=ABCP.GMSTR(+1),
//              DISP=(NEW,CATLG,DELETE),
//              UNIT=SYSDA,               DASD
//              VOL=SER=TSO001, ...
```

2.2.5. DD Format—SPACE

```
//  SPACE=(type,(#1,#2[,#3])[,RLSE][,CONTIG][,ROUND])
    TRK,
    CYL,        [,index]        [,MXIG]
    blksize,                    [,ALX]
    reclgth,                    [,]
```

DD Parameter—SPACE

• *SPACE* gives size of data set when writing to DASD. SPACE is coded in block size, cylinders, and tracks or in an SMS environment by number of records.

• *Type* allows user to request space using one of the following parameters: TRK, CYL, blksize, or record-length (SMS only).

  • #1—Gives the initial allocation or primary space—code 25% more than needed.

  • #2—Gives this quantity 15 times if needed. User should code about 10% to 20% of primary.

  • #3—Creates directories for PDS members; one directory allows about 6 members.

• When asking for space using tracks or cylinders, user needs to figure the number of records that fit in a block. Then determine the number of blocks that fit on a track.

  ☞ *See: DASD Capacity.*

• With SMS user can ask for space in number of records. This is preferred, as it gives device independence.

  ☞ *See: SMS below.*

• Index—Gives number of tracks for index of indexed sequential data set; must be 1 or more cylinders.

• RLSE—Releases unused space when closed. The lowest value the system releases is tracks. System releases in cylinders when space is requested in cylinders.

• CONTIG—Insists primary space must be adjoining or job fails with a space ABEND. This is an older coding technique.

• ROUND—Allocates to nearest cylinder when space request is in block size, then allocates on cylinder boundaries.

- MXIG—Allocates primary space to largest contiguous area on volume if area is as big or bigger than space requested.

- ALX—Allocates primary to five largest contiguous areas on volume if area is as big or bigger than the space requested.

SPACE Request in Tracks—Example 1

```
//MSTRO      DD  DSN=ABCP.GMSTR(+1),
//               DISP=(NEW,CATLG,DELETE),
//               UNIT=SYSDA,
//               SPACE=(TRK,(1500,150),RLSE),
//               DCB=(RECFM=FB,LRECL=80,BLKSIZE=23440)
```

SPACE Request in Cylinders—Example 2

```
//MSTRO      DD  DSN=ABCP.SIMPLE,
//               DISP=(NEW,CATLG,DELETE),
//               UNIT=SYSDA,
//               SPACE=(CYL,(100,10),RLSE),
//               DCB=(RECFM=FB,LRECL=80,BLKSIZE=23440)
```

SPACE Request in Blocks—Example 3

```
//...
//               SPACE=(23440,(3000,300),RLSE,,ROUND),
//               DCB=(RECFM=FB,LRECL=80,BLKSIZE=23440)
```

- Examples above request the same amount of space.

  ☞ **See:** SMS below.

2.2.6. ESA Space Allocation

- PDS and direct access data sets—System limits to one volume.

- Sequential data set—System allocates primary within 5 extents on one volume (system tries to get a continuous area big enough to hold the primary).

- The 11-15 remaining secondary extents, if needed, are put on same volume if space is available.

- If more space is needed and enough space cannot be found on the same volume, or all 16 extents are used, then the system goes to another volume.

- The system can use up to 5 volumes, each with up to 16 extents. Previous to ESA, the system used only 1 volume with up to 16 extents.

2.2.7. DD Format—DCB

```
// DCB=(model.dscb,RECFM=x,LRECL=#,BLKSIZE=##)
```

DD Parameters—DCB

- DCB—gives Data Control Block characteristics such as size of record, record format, and block size.

- DCB information comes from the following in the order presented. If the information is conflicting, an error occurs.

  1) Program.

  2) JCL.

  3) Data set label.

  4) MVS defaults.

- RECFM—Gives the type of file being created. Commonly used values for RECFM are:

  - FB|VB—Assigns fixed or variable blocked data set characteristics.

  - FBA|VBA—Controls spacing on printed output by placing an ASA character in column 1 of every record.

  - VS|VBS—Means one record spans two or more blocks.

  - U—Indicates record format is undefined. An example of an undefined type of data set would be a load library.

- LRECL— Gives record length of data set in bytes.

- BLKSIZE—Determines how data set is written to the device. For medium and large data sets a larger block size uses less media and reduces I/O. The largest block size is 32760 or 32764 for variable blocked. To figure block size for DASD, user must know the number of bytes per track. With ESA and higher releases let the system determine block size. System blocks DASD at half track, and tape at 32K.

- System copies block size from model data set if used. User can code BLKSIZE = 0 in the JCL. This forces the system to figure block size; then system doesn't copy block size from the model.

- When possible, do not specify block size in program for COBOL programs, code—BLOCK CONTAINS 0 RECORDS.

Calculate Block Size Tape Data Set (Older Coding Technique)

- Fixed—To figure for tape (if LRECL=80 then take 32760/80=409 drop remainder 409x80=32720).

- Variable—(largest LRECL + 4 bytes = 84 32000/84 = 380, drop remainder 380x84 = 31920 + 4 = <u>31924</u>), must add 4 because it is VB.

  ☞ *See: DASD Capacity and ESA BLKSIZE.*

- DCB=model.dataset—a pre existing model data set is required as the first subparameter of the DCB when creating a +1 GDS. *P.MODL* is the name for the model data set in the examples below.

- A systems programmer usually creates the model data sets.

  ☞ *See: SMS Example 5 the model data set is not needed with SMS.*

DD Output Format

```
//ddname2   DD   DSN=data.set.name,
//                DISP=(begin,normal-step,abend-step),
//                UNIT=unitname,
//                SPACE=(type,(primary,secondary),RLSE),
//                DCB=(model.dscb,RECFM=x,LRECL=#,BLKSIZE=##)
```

- SPACE parameter is coded when writing to DASD only

DD Output Simple Data Set—Example 1
(Older Coding Technique)

```
//MSTRO     DD   DSN=ABCP.SIMPLE,
//                DISP=(NEW,CATLG,DELETE),
//                UNIT=SYSDA,
//                SPACE=(CYL,(20,4),RLSE),
//                DCB=(LRECL=80,RECFM=FB,BLKSIZE=6160)
```

DD Output for GDS (+1)—Example 2
(Older Coding Technique)

```
//MSTRO     DD   DSN=ABCP.GMSTR(+1),
//                DISP=(NEW,CATLG,DELETE),
//                UNIT=SYSDA,
//                SPACE=(CYL,(20,4),RLSE),
//                DCB=(P.MODL,LRECL=80,RECFM=FB,BLKSIZE=6160)
```

DD Output Simple Data Set—Example 3 (ESA)

```
//MSTRO     DD  DSN=ABCP.SIMPLE,
//              DISP=(NEW,CATLG,DELETE),
//              UNIT=SYSDA,
//              SPACE=(CYL,(20,4),RLSE),
//              LRECL=80,RECFM=FB
```

DD Output for GDS (+1)—Example 4 (ESA)

```
//MSTRO     DD  DSN=ABCP.GMSTR(+1),
//              DISP=(NEW,CATLG,DELETE),
//              UNIT=SYSDA,
//              SPACE=(CYL,(20,4),RLSE),
//              DCB=(P.MODL,LRECL=80,RECFM=FB,BLKSIZE=0)
```

- With ESA, BLKSIZE and DCB are not needed. Try coding BLKSIZE=0 when a block size is required to force system to block.

DD Output for GDS (+1)—Example 5 (SMS)

```
//MSTRO     DD  DSN=ABCP.GMSTR(+1),
//              DISP=(NEW,CATLG,DELETE),
//              UNIT=SYSDA,
//              SPACE=(CYL,(20,4),RLSE),
//              LRECL=80,RECFM=FB
```

- Model DSCB is not needed in an SMS environment.

  ☞ **See:** *ESA and AVGREC (SMS).*

  ☞ **See:** *When to Code DD Parameters LABEL (i.e., using tape, do not code space).*

2.2.8. SYSIN—Reads Control Statements

SYSIN—Format 1

```
//SYSIN    DD  *
     control statements
/*
```

SYSIN—Format 2

```
//SYSIN    DD  DATA,DLM=xx
     control statements
xx
```

* DD * or DD DATA—Indicates in stream data or control statements follow. Must use DD DATA if in–stream data contain JCL statements. Control statements must be 80 bytes long, or job abends with wrong length record.

* /* or xx—End of data. If /* is not coded, the system knows end of data when it reads the next JCL statement. User defines the value for xx. This format must be used if the data contains JCL statements.

2.2.9. SYSOUT—Printed Output

SYSOUT—Format

```
//ddname3   DD   SYSOUT=(x,pgm-id,formid),
//               COPIES=#,
//               DEST=dest,
//               OUTLIM=lines,
//               FCB=(image,[ALIGN|VERIFY]),
//               HOLD=[NO|YES]
```

SYSOUT Parameter

- SYSOUT=x—Gives report or message print class.

- SYSOUT=*—Copies value from MSGCLASS.

- SYSOUT=(,)—Nullifies print class.

- Pgm-id—Identifies special program to write output.

- Formid—Gives 4-character special form id.

- COPIES=#—Creates x number of reports up to 254.

- DEST=dest—Routes to specific location.

- OUTLIM=#—Limits number of lines printed.

- Image—Gives image of up to 4 alphanumeric or national characters.

- ALIGN—Asks operator to check that forms are in line.

- VERIFY—Checks print image and asks operator to check that forms are in line.

- HOLD=YES—Holds output until released.

- Hold=NO—Processes normally (default if HOLD is not coded).

SYSOUT Examples—Printed Output

```
//PRTOUT   DD   SYSOUT=A,
//               COPIES=2
```

- Route 2 copies of the report to print class A.

```
//PAY1R    DD   SYSOUT=(A,,1234)
```

- Request special form 1234 to be mounted.

SYSOUT—Print Program Display

```
//SYSOUT    DD    SYSOUT=*
```

- SYSOUT in columns 3-10 prints application program displays upon printer and messages from the SORT utility.

- * Means use value from the MSGCLASS parameter.

SYSPRINT—Print Utility Messages

```
//SYSPRINT DD    SYSOUT=*
```

- SYSPRINT in columns 3-10 prints utility messages such as IDCAMS, IEBGENER, etc.

SYSDBOUT—Print COBOL II Formatted Dump

```
//SYSDBOUT  DD    SYSOUT=D          FORMATTED DUMP
//SYSABOUT  DD    SYSOUT=*          BASE LOCATORS
```

- SYSDBOUT in columns 3-10 prints COBOL II formatted Dump.

SYSUDUMP —Application Program Dump

```
//SYSUDUMP  DD    SYSOUT=D
```

- SYSUDUMP in columns 3-10 prints the application program dump.

SYSOUT Processing Order

- Here's the order of processing parameters from highest to lowest:

  1) SYSOUT DD

  2) Explicit (OUTPUT=*.name)

  3) Step Implicit (after EXEC PGM)

  4) Job Implicit (after JOB)

2.2.10. DUMMY—Ignore Input or Output DD

- DUMMY means I/O processes and JCL parameters coded on the data set are ignored. If reading a data set, the result is an end of file.

- System might need a block size when DUMMY is coded on a physical sequential data set so the open can get buffers.

- If data sets are concatenated, system ignores all data sets after DUMMY.

  See: Data Set Concatenation.

Non-ESA DUMMY Format

```
//ddname    DD  DUMMY,
//              DCB=BLKSIZE=lrecl
```

ESA—DUMMY Format

```
//ddname    DD  DUMMY,BLKSIZE=lrecl
```

- DCB keyword is not needed.

```
//ddname    DD  DUMMY,AMP=AMORG
```

- Assign to VSAM, then AMP=AMORG is needed. AMORG is Access Method ORGanization.

NULLFILE Format

```
//ddname    DD  DSN=NULLFILE,
//              DISP=SHR
```

- NULLFILE is an alternative to coding DD DUMMY. DUMMY is more commonly used.

2.3. EXEC PGM STATEMENT

- EXEC PGM statement provides the load module to execute for each job step. Parameters typically coded here are:

- PARM to pass data to the program.

- COND to check for previous successful step execution before running this step.

  ☞ Suggest coding COND on every step except the first step, as there is nothing to check.

- The data sets used by the program are defined using data definition statements. The DDs follow the EXEC PGM.

EXEC PGM Format

```
//stepname EXEC PGM=pgmname,
//              PARM=('pgm-data'),
//              COND=(#,oper),
//              REGION=sizeK|M,
//              TIME=(minutes,seconds)|1440,
//              ACCT=(step-acctinfo)
```

- Pgmname—Names the load module to run. There's a limit of 255 per job.

  👌 *See: Three Ways to Code JCL, for placement.*

- PARM—Passes up to 100 characters to the program. This includes any commas passed to the program, but does not include parentheses or apostrophes, since they are part of the syntax. Special characters must be enclosed in apostrophes.

- COND *—Controls step execution. Checks for a valid return code—highest return code from all previous steps. For example, a return code of "0" typically means the run was successful. User can also code step specific checks.

---

* *ACCT, COND, REGION, and TIME can be coded on JOB statement for all steps in job. System ignores what is coded on EXEC PGM statement and uses what is coded on JOB statement.*

☞   Suggest avoiding step specific checks unless they are really needed.

☞   Suggest coding the newer IF statement instead of COND as the logic is easier to understand.

&ᐰ   **See:** *IF/THEN/ELSE/ENDIF, ESA.*

- REGION*

&ᐰ   **See:** *JOB Statement.*

- TIME*

&ᐰ   **See:** *JOB Statement.*

- ACCT*

&ᐰ   **See:** *JOB Statement.*

☞   Suggest coding REGION, TIME, and ACCT on JOB statement if needed. Reduces confusion and promotes easier maintenance.

2.3.1. EXEC PGM Format—PARM

```
//stepname EXEC PGM=pgmname,
//              PARM=('pgm-data')

//...
```

COBOL PARM Example

```
LINKAGE SECTION.
01  PARM-IN.
    05  PARM-LNGTH        PIC  S9(4)  BINARY.
    05  COMPANY           PIC  X(04).
    05  FILLER            PIC  X.
    05  RUN               PIC  X.

    PROCEDURE  DIVISION    USING  PARM-IN.
```

• Shows how to code a COBOL program to accept a JCL PARM.

JCL PARM Example

```
//UPDAT050 EXEC PGM=xxxxxxxx,
//              PARM='MVST,M'
```

• Shows how to code PARM input for above COBOL program. Enclose special characters in apostrophes.

COBOL Compile PARM Continuation Example

```
//UPDAT050 EXEC PGM=xxxxxxxx,
//              PARM=('COMPILE,DATA(31),FLAG(I,E)',
//              'LIB,MAP,OFFSET,NUMPROC(MIG),RENT')
```

• To continue a PARM, enclose each line in apostrophes and entire PARM in parentheses.

2.3.2. EXEC PGM Format—COND

```
//              COND=(#,oper)
//              COND=(#,oper[,stepname])
```

COND Parameter

- COND parameter checks whether previous step(s) ran OK, then runs this step. Expression is COND=(#,oper). Result(s) must be FALSE for step to run.

  &ℐ *See: Return Code Table.*

- Up to eight expressions can be coded.

  oper: EQ|NE|LT|LE|GT|GE

  #:   0 to 4095

COND—All Previous Steps Format

```
//stepname EXEC PGM=pgmname,
//              COND=(#,oper)
```

- Checks highest return code from all previous steps.

COND—All Previous Steps Example

```
//PS020      EXEC PGM=ABCPGM,
//              COND=(4,LT)
```

- PS020 runs if previous steps received return codes of 0-4.

COND—Specific Step(s) Format

```
//              COND=(#,oper[,stepname])
```

- Checks return code from step specified.

COND—Specific Step(s) and Example

```
//PS010      EXEC PGM=XYZPGM
...
//PS040      EXEC PGM=ABCPGM,
//              COND=(4,LT,PS010)
```

- PS040 runs if step PS010 received a return code of 0-4.

COND—Specific Step(s) Multiple PROCs Format

```
//              COND=(#,oper[,jobstepname.procstepname])
```

- Checks return code from step specified. Jobstepname is found in columns 3-10 of EXEC PROC. Procstepname is found in columns 3-10 of EXEC PGM.

COND—Specific Step(s) Multiple PROCs Example

```
//STEP01    EXEC PROC=ABCPROC
//STEP02    EXEC PROC=ABCPROC2
//

//ABCPROC       PROC
//PS010      EXEC PGM=XYZPGM
...
//ABCPROC2      PROC
//PS020      EXEC PGM=ABCPGM,
//                COND=(4,LT,STEP01.PS010)
```

- PS020 runs if STEP01.PS010 received a return code of 0-4.

COND—Multiple Expressions Format

```
//                COND=((#,oper),(#,oper))
```

- Enclose expressions within parentheses, separate multiple expressions with a comma, and enclose in parentheses.

COND—Multiple Expressions Example

```
//PS010      EXEC PGM=XYZPGM
...
//PS100      EXEC PGM=ABCPGM,
//                COND=((4,LT),(0,NE,PS010))
```

- If any step gets a return code greater than 4, PS100 does not run. Likewise, if step PS010 gets a return code greater than 0, PS100 does not run. If either condition is met, step does not run.

2.3.3. EXEC PGM Format—REGION

```
//                REGION=sizeK|M,
```

2.3.4. EXEC PGM FORMAT—TIME

```
//                TIME=(minutes,seconds)|1440,
```

REGION and TIME Example

```
//UPDAT050 EXEC PGM=xxxxxxxx,
//                REGION=4096K,
//                TIME=(4,30)     *LIMIT 4MIN 30SEC
```

- REGION specifies an upper limit of storage to run the job. TIME limits CPU time to 4 minutes, 30 seconds.

☞ Suggest coding REGION and TIME on JOB statement if needed.

2.4. EXEC PROC STATEMENT

• EXEC PROC statement calls cataloged procedure (procname) to run.

  ✍ **See:** *Three Ways to Code JCL, for placement.*

• Two ways to code EXEC PROC statement are depicted in the following examples. Preferred method is to code the PROC= so there is no confusion as to what is being executed.

EXEC PROC Format 1

```
//jobstep  EXEC PROC=procname
```

• Include the keyword PROC to clarify what is being executed.

EXEC PROC Example 1

```
//JS0001   EXEC PROC=PAYW010
```

EXEC PROC Format 2

```
//jobstep  EXEC procname
```

• Keyword PROC is not coded. The default in OS/390 is to execute a PROC. While in DOS/VSE the default is to execute a program.

  ☞   Suggest coding PROC keyword for clarity.

EXEC PROC Example 2

```
//JS0001   EXEC PAYW010
```

2.5. IF/THEN/ELSE/ENDIF* STATEMENT

- IF/THEN/ELSE/ENDIF statement controls step execution. This statement checks whether previous step(s) ran successfully, then runs this step. Expression is (RC oper #). Result(s) must be TRUE for step to run.

- When IF expression is true the step following the IF runs. When IF is not true, step following the ELSE runs.

☞ Suggest coding this statement instead of COND parameter as it is newer coding and easier to understand.

☞ Suggest not coding name in columns 3-10 of IF...ENDIF. Code one IF...ENDIF per step as each step should contain a return code check. Do not code both the IF statement and the COND parameter. Choose 1 way and use that method consistently within the job JCL.

See: Return Code Table.

- Code IF . . . THEN before EXEC PGM statement. Code ELSE and ENDIF after last DD of step. Must code IF (expression), THEN JCL statements, followed by ENDIF. ELSE is not required.

    oper: EQ|NE|LT|LE|GT|GE|AND|NOT|OR

    #:   0 to 4095

IF/THEN/ELSE/ENDIF Format

```
//[name]    IF  (keyword  oper  #)  THEN [comments]
//[name]    EXEC PGM=pgmname
//ddname    DD ...
[//         ELSE       [comments]
//[name]    EXEC PGM=pgmname
//ddname    DD ...]
//[name]    ENDIF      [comments]
```

IF/THEN/ELSE/ENDIF Example

```
//          IF  (RC  LT  5)  THEN
//PS020     EXEC PGM=pgmname
//DDAIN     DD  DSN=dataset.name,
...
//          ELSE
//PS030     EXEC PGM=pgmname
//DDXIN     DD  DSN=dataset.name2,
...
//          ENDIF
```

- Step PS020 runs if previous steps highest return code was 0-4. If PS020 does not run due to return code check, then PS030 runs.

  &✐ **See:** COND Compare with IF ... ENDIF.

Expression Keywords

RC	Tests Return Code(s)
ABEND[=<u>TRUE</u>]	Tests if abend occurred
¬ABEND|ABEND=FALSE	Tests for no abend occurred
ABENDCC=S|Ucode	Tests for specific system code or user code
	S = System
	U = User codes
RUN[=<u>TRUE</u>]	Tests whether a <u>specific</u> step ran
¬RUN|RUN=FALSE	Tests if <u>specific</u> step didn't run

Check Highest RC All Previous Steps Format

```
//[name]     IF  (keyword oper  #)  THEN  [comments]
//step#      EXEC PGM=pgmname
//ddname     DD ...
//[name]     ENDIF
```

Check Highest RC All Previous Steps Example

```
//          IF  (RC LE 4) THEN     *TRUE RUN
//PS020     EXEC PGM=pgmname
//ddname    DD  DSN=dataset.name,
...
//          ENDIF
```

- Step PS020 runs if previous steps highest return code was 0-4.

Specific Step Format

```
//step#      EXEC PGM=pgmname
...
//[name]     IF  (step#.RC oper #)   THEN [comments]
//step#2     EXEC PGM=pgmname
//ddname     DD  ...
```

Specific Step Example

```
//PS010      EXEC PGM=pgmname
...
//           IF  (PS010.RC  LT  5)  THEN
//PS020      EXEC PGM=pgmname
//ddname     DD  DSN=dataset.name,
...
//           ENDIF
```

- Step PS020 runs if PS010 received a return code of 0-4.

IF . . . ENDIF Specific Step Rule

- When using specific step format, if specific step does not run, result is FALSE. Therefore, if a specific step is used, the following should be coded to allow step restart or the system will not let the user restart the job in that step.

- System does, however, allow a restart of a COND specific step check. This is how the system differs with respect to resolving step specific checks using the COND parameter.

```
OR  (STEP#.RUN  EQ  FALSE)
```

Specific Step and FALSE to Allow Step Restart Example

```
//PS010      EXEC PGM=XYZPGM
//           IF  ((PS010.RC  EQ  0)  OR
//               (PS010.RUN  EQ  FALSE))  THEN
//PS020      EXEC PGM=ABCPGM
//ddname     DD  DSN=dataset.name,
...
//           ENDIF
```

Specific Step(s) Multiple PROCs Format

```
//          IF (jobstep.step#.RC  oper  #)  THEN
```

Specific Step(s) Multiple PROCs Example

```
//STEP01    EXEC PROC=ABCPROC
//STEP02    EXEC PROC=ABCPROC2
//

//ABCPROC   PROC
//PS010     EXEC PGM=XYZPGM
...

//ABCPROC2 PROC
//          IF (STEP01.PS010.RC LT 4) THEN
//PS020     EXEC PGM=ABCPGM
//ddname    DD  DSN=dataset.name,
...
//          ENDIF
```

- Checks specific step from another PROC within the job run.

IF/THEN/ENDIF Check for User Abend Example

```
//          IF (ABENDCC  EQ  U0099)  THEN
//PS030     EXEC PGM=pgmname
//DDXIN     DD  DSN=dataset.name,
...
//          ENDIF
```

- Checks most recent user ABEND code.

IF/THEN/ENDIF Check for System Abend Example

```
//          IF (ABENDCC  EQ  S0C7)  THEN
//PS030     EXEC PGM=pgmname
//DDXIN     DD  DSN=dataset.name,
...
//          ENDIF
```

- Checks most recent system ABEND code.

2.6. JCLLIB* STATEMENT

- JCLLIB statement names the libraries to search for PROCLIB and or INCLUDEd member(s). This statement is limited to one per job. Code after JOB statement or any JES statements and before the EXEC PROC statement.

- To continue, break at comma and start next line in columns 4-16. This can be used instead of the JES2 statement: /*JOBPARM PROCLIB= ... An advantage is that a PROCLIB no longer has to be defined to JES2 PROC when using the JCLLIB statement.

  See: JES2 PROC Appendix B.

  ☞ Suggest coding JCLLIB instead of JOBPARM to tell system where to find the PROC.

JCLLIB Format

```
//[name]    JCLLIB ORDER=(library1[,    [comment]
//                library2,library3])    [comment]
```

JCLLIB Example

```
//           JCLLIB ORDER=(PROD.PROCLIB,TEST.PROCLIB)
```

- Search PROD.PROCLIB, then TEST.PROCLIB for the PROC. If not found, search system default libraries.

  See: JES2 PROC Appendix B.

---

* *JCLLIB -- JES2 V4 & MVS/ESA V4.*

2.7. JOB STATEMENT

* JOB statement provides job name and run information. There is one JOB statement per job. It must be coded first.

* Exceptions include:

  * JES2 statements for command and PRIORITY—that are not allowed at most shops.

  * //*%OPC statements used with IBM's OPC scheduling software. Check to see what scheduling software your shop is using.

  See: Statement Names, jobname.

JOB Format

```
1                  1   1
                   2   6
//jobname   JOB (accounting),'programmer name',
//              CLASS=x,
//              MSGCLASS=x,
//              MSGLEVEL=(1,1),
//              NOTIFY=logonid,
//              PRTY=#,
//              REGION=sizeK|M,
//              RESTART=jobstep.procstep|stepname,
//              TIME=(minutes,seconds)|1440,
//              TYPRUN=HOLD|SCAN
```

JOB Statement Parameters

* (accounting)—Gives charge back information. Can be positional and must be coded after the keyword JOB with a maximum of 142 characters.

* 'Programmer name'—Gives brief job description of production and often contains user's name and phone for test environment. Can be positional and must be coded after accounting with a maximum of 20 characters. This prints on banner page and can be used for distribution with test jobs.

* COND

  See: EXEC PGM Statement.

- CLASS—Gives initiator where job runs, on a first-in first-out basis. To display default information about a class, use the JES2 command.

  ☞ *See: JES2 Job Class Display Appendix C.*

  $DJOBCLASS(x)

- MSGCLASS—Indicates output print class where JCL statements and messages print.

- MSGLEVEL—Allows user to print JCL statements and messages: 0 is off and 1 is on.

  ☞ Suggest coding if the default is not 1,1. 1,1 means print all JCL statements and messages if job completes normally, also if job abends.

- NOTIFY—Sends job-ended message to user. Used when testing jobs.

- PRTY=#—Changes first-in first-out order in the input queue. The # is a number from 1-15, with 15 being the highest priority. Should not be coded, as everyone would code; then there would be no priority. Also, the system is set up to ignore PRTY at many shops.

- REGION*—Gives an upper limit for storage needed to run job. Use if system default is too small: K—*kilobyte* gives 1024 bytes; M—*megabyte* gives 1024 kilobytes (4096K or 4M is a good starting point). If a region ABEND appears, such as 80A or 106, a quick fix is to code 0K or 0M, which allows an upper limit of all available storage above and below the 16MB line.

  ☞ *See: Job output message IEF374I (to figure region used by the job run).*

---

* *ACCT, COND, REGION, and TIME can be coded on JOB statement for all steps in job. System ignores what is coded on EXEC PGM statement and uses what is coded on JOB statement.*

- RESTART—Allows specific step rerun. Job step is found in columns 3–10 on EXEC PROC statement; PROC step is found in columns 3–10 on EXEC PGM statement. Step name is found in columns 3–10 on EXEC PGM for "Plain or simple JCL"–JCL that is not in a PROC format.

  ☞ **See:** *Three Ways To Code JCL.*

- TIME*—Limits or extends CPU time. Default is usually determined by the CLASS. CLASS is defined by the shop's systems group. System ABEND 322 means job exceeded CPU time. Time=1440 gives unlimited CPU time.

  ☞ **See:** *JES2 job class display, Appendix C.*

  ☞ **See:** *TIME, ESA.*

  ☞ Suggest coding REGION and TIME on the JOB statement if needed, not the EXEC PGM. Parameters coded on the job statement override parameters coded on the EXEC PGM statement.

- TYPRUN=HOLD—Means operator must release job to run.

  ☞ Suggest not coding in production JCL when using an automated scheduling software package.

- TYPRUN=SCAN—Checks for JCL syntax errors. Job does not run.

RESTART PROC Format

```
//jobname  JOB (acct-info),'job desc',
//            CLASS=x,
//            MSGCLASS=x,
//            RESTART=jobstep.procstep
//jobstep  EXEC PROC=procname
//

//procname PROC
//procstep EXEC PGM=pgmname
...
```

---

* *ACCT, COND, REGION, and TIME can be coded on JOB statement for all steps in job. System ignores what is coded on EXEC PGM statement and uses what is coded on JOB statement.*

RESTART Plain JCL Format

```
//jobname   JOB … ,
//              RESTART=step#
//step#      EXEC PGM=pgmname
```

JOB Examples

Basic Production JOB Example 1

```
//PAYW010   JOB (PAY,1234),'PRINT PAY CHECKS',
//          CLASS=P,
//          MSGCLASS=M
```

• Accounting, brief job description, CLASS and MSGCLASS are typically required at most facilities.

Basic Test JOB Example 2

```
//TPGMAOD1 JOB (TEST,DEPT10),'ANN O.DRYDEN 2222',
//          CLASS=A,
//          MSGCLASS=X,
//          NOTIFY=TPGMAOD
```

• Test job names typically contain the user's TSO logon plus 1 character, along with CLASS, MSGCLASS and NOTIFY to let the user know the job completed.

Test JOB with HOLD Example 3

```
//TPGMAOD1 JOB (TEST,DEPT10),'ANN O.DRYDEN 2222',
//          CLASS=A,
//          MSGCLASS=X,
//          TYPRUN=HOLD,
//          NOTIFY=TPGMAOD
```

• Test job with HOLD. Job sits in the input queue typically until operations releases the job. Sometimes used to control when long running test jobs are executed.

REGION Example 4

```
//PAYW010   JOB (PAY,1234),'PRINT PAY CHECKS',
//          CLASS=P,
//          MSGCLASS=M,
//          REGION=8M    *SETS UPPER LIMIT
//JS001     EXEC PROC=PAYW010P
//
```

• REGION sets an upper limit of 8 megabytes of storage as comment denotes.

RESTART at First Step Example 5

```
//              RESTART=*  START AT 1ST STEP
```

- Value of * indicates restart at 1st step as comments state.

RESTART PROC Example 6

```
//PAYW010   JOB (PAY,1234),'PRINT PAY CHECKS',
//              CLASS=P,
//              MSGCLASS=M,
//              RESTART=JS001.PS050
//JS001     EXEC PROC=PAYW010
//

//PAYW010   PROC
//PS010     EXEC PGM=PGM1
...
//PS050     EXEC PGM=PGM99
```

- Job step name is found in columns 3-10 of EXEC PROC statement. PROC step name is found in columns 3-10 of EXEC PGM statement.

- RESTART job in PROC step PS050.

RESTART Plain JCL Example 7

```
//TWEBER1   JOB (BIL,1234),'BRITTANI 2222',
//              CLASS=A,
//              MSGCLASS=X,
//              NOTIFY=TWEBER,
//**GEN020 COLS 3-10 ON EXEC PGM **
//              RESTART=GEN020
//* * * * * * * * * * * * * * * * * * * * * * * * *
//UPDAT05   EXEC PGM=xxx
//ddname    DD ...
//* * * * * * * * * * * * * * * * * * * * * * * * *
//GEN020    EXEC PGM=IEBGENER ...
```

- RESTART job in step GEN020.

2.8. JOBLIB STATEMENT

- JOBLIB statement specifies library to search for job's load modules. Code JOBLIB right after JOB statement or JES statements (if JES statements are used).

- If JOBLIB and STEPLIB are coded, STEPLIB is used for that step and JOBLIB is ignored by the system.

- System searches system defaults if load module is not found in library specified by JOBLIB or STEPLIB. Application programs are usually not found here, so JOBLIB or STEPLIB must be coded.

☞ Suggest using JOBLIB, as it is easier to maintain.

Data Set Concatenation

- User specifies more than one input data set by coding DD name on the first DD, but do not code DD name on the rest of the DDs. Can't mix tape and DASD. Must specify the data set with the largest block size first, except for ESA.

☞ *See: Concatenation, for ESA.*

JOBLIB Format with Concatenation

```
//JOBLIB    DD   DSN=library1,     (SEARCH 1ST)
//               DISP=SHR
//          DD   DSN=library2,     (SEARCH 2ND)
//               DISP=SHR
```

JOBLIB Example with Concatenation

```
//JOBLIB    DD   DSN=PFIX.LOADLIB,  (SEARCH  1ST)
//               DISP=SHR
//          DD   DSN=PROD.LOADLIB,  (SEARCH  2ND)
//               DISP=SHR
```

- Searches PFIX.LOADLIB then PROD.LOADLIB for the application load module. If not found, program abends with a system 806 error.

2.9. NULL STATEMENT

- NULL statement indicates end of JCL. Format is: // then blanks in columns 3-72. The NULL statement cannot be coded in a PROC, except ESA V4.

    See: NULL statement, ESA.

NULL Format and Example

    //

2.10. OUTPUT STATEMENT

- OUTPUT statement specifies the same parameters found on the SYSOUT DD or can be used to add functions not available on the SYSOUT DD. Code parameters in any order. User can code up to 128 OUTPUT statements.

Refer Back Formats

- OUTPUT statement(s) must be coded before SYSOUT(s) referring to the OUTPUT statement.

    ```
    *.OUTname
       or
    *.stepname.OUTname
       or
    *.jobstepname.stepname.OUTname
    ```

- OUT name is found in columns 3-10 of OUTPUT statement.

- Step name is found in columns 3-10 of EXEC PGM in "Plain JCL".

- Job step name is found in columns 3-10 of EXEC PROC statement and PROC step name is found in columns 3-10 of EXEC PGM in cataloged procedures.

OUTPUT Explicit Format—Points to OUTPUT (Refer Back)

```
//namex      OUTPUT parameter[,parameter] ...
//ddname     DD  SYSOUT=x,OUTPUT=*.namex
```

OUTPUT JCL Statement Example

```
//OUT1       OUTPUT CLASS=A,COPIES=2
//OUT2       OUTPUT CLASS=B,DEST=DEPA
//REPT1      DD  SYSOUT=(,),OUTPUT=(*.OUT1,*.OUT2)
```

* SYSOUT=(,) nullifies output. The OUT1 DD prints two copies in class A; then, with the OUT2 DD, a third copy prints in class B at another location—DEPA.

OUTPUT Implicit—Code After JOB or EXEC PGM

```
//name       OUTPUT DEFAULT=Y,parameter ...
```

* If OUTPUT is coded after JOB, it applies to whole job. If it is coded after EXEC PGM, it applies to that step.

* Y—Means OUTPUT is implicitly referenced by SYSOUTs and cannot be referred to explicitly (e.g., //name   OUTPUT DEFAULT=[N|Y],parameter. . .).

* N—Means OUTPUT must be referred to explicitly. This is the default.

2.11. PROC STATEMENT

* PROC statement identifies the beginning of the PROC.

  ⌖ *See: Three Ways to Code JCL, for placement.*

PROC Format

```
//procname PROC
```

Example

```
//ABCPROC    PROC
//PS010      EXEC PGM=...
```

2.12. SET* STATEMENT

- SET statement assigns a value to a symbolic, e.g., &symbolic whenever the system comes to a SET statement.

    ☞ *See: Symbolic.*

- SET statements can be coded anywhere in the JCL and in any type of JCL (e.g., "Plain JCL"). Values are assigned when the job runs. SET is not affected by IF ... ENDIF logic.

    ☞ Suggest using SET with plain JCL only. Do not code SET in a PROC, as SET values within a PROC cannot be overridden.

SET Format—Plain JCL

```
//[name]    SET symbolic='value1'[,
//              symbolic2='value2']...
//jobstep  EXEC PGM=pgmname
//STEPLIB  DD  DSN=&symbolic..dataset...
```

SET Example—Plain JCL

```
//TBRITT2   JOB (BIL,1234),'BRITTANI 2222',
//              CLASS=A,
//              MSGCLASS=X,
//              NOTIFY=TBRITT
//* * * * * * * * * * * * * * * * * * * *
//            SET LIB='TEST'
//stepname EXEC PGM=pgmname
//STEPLIB  DD  DSN=&LIB..LOADLIB,
//              DISP=SHR
...
```

- When plain JCL runs, system substitutes: TEST.LOADLIB

SET Format—PROC

```
//procname PROC
//[name]    SET  symbolic='value3'[,
//              symbolic2='value4']...
//stepname EXEC PGM=pgmname
//STEPLIB  DD  DSN=&symbolic..dataset...
```

---

* *SET -- MVS/ESA V4.*

SET Example—PROC

```
//procname PROC
//         SET LIB='PROD'
//stepname EXEC PGM=pgmname
//         SET LIB='TEST'
//STEPLIB  DD  DSN=&LIB..LOADLIB...
```

- When PROC runs, system substitutes: TEST.LOADLIB
- The system uses the value on the last SET statement.

  ☞ Suggest not using SET in a PROC because the user cannot override the symbolic value. Code symbolic using the older coding for PROCs to allow symbolic overrides.

  ✍ **See:** *Symbolic.*

2.13. STEPLIB STATEMENT

- A STEPLIB statement specifies which private library to search for the load module (e.g., EXEC PGM=load-module).

- When JOBLIB and STEPLIB are coded, STEPLIB is used and JOBLIB is ignored.

- If STEPLIB is used for consistency, code after EXEC PGM in each step. This is not needed for programs in system libraries (e.g., IDCAMS, IBM Utilities).

  ☞ Suggest using JOBLIB instead because it is easier to maintain.

  ✍ *See: Data Set Concatenation.*

STEPLIB Format

```
//procstep EXEC PGM=loadname
//STEPLIB  DD  DSN=load.module.library,
//             DISP=SHR    *CODE SHR FOR LIBRARIES
```

STEPLIB Example

```
//PS010    EXEC PGM=PAY500
//STEPLIB  DD  DSN=PROD.LOADLIB,
//             DISP=SHR      *SHR FOR LIBRARIES
//DDIN     DD  DSN=…
//PS020    EXEC PGM=PAY500
//STEPLIB  DD  DSN=PROD.LOADLIB, *CODE EVERY STEP
//             DISP=SHR
```

- System locates load modules PAY500, and PAY800 in PROD.LOADLIB.

  ☞ Suggest for system 806 abend "load module not found", check to see if program name was spelled correctly, or if module was moved into the proper library.

Syntax of SMS Parameters **3**

Storage Management Subsystem (SMS) is IBM's concept for facilitating DASD management. SMS provides control during the initial allocation of data sets. SMS can be set up to manage space allocation and data set placement, along with how long data sets reside on DASD.

The storage administrator sets up rules to manage data sets based on the type of data set such as:

- Production versus test.

- On-line versus batch.

Using these rules the system automatically migrates the data set to tape based upon the type of data set and the last time the data set was accessed. For instance, on-line data sets would not be migrated. Test data sets would be migrated if they are not accessed for x number of days.

User can view the Interactive Storage Management Facility (ISMF) on-line to see how SMS is set up at their site.

SMS must be functional to allow the user to code SMS parameters. The parameters are typically coded on the DD statement for DASD data sets.

Parameters are listed in alphabetical order and include the following.

AVGREC—Asks for space in number of records. Easier for user because the user no longer has to calculate space and AVGREC promotes device independence.

DATACLAS—Supplies data class data set characteristics such as space, record length, etc.

DSNTYPE—Indicates an improved new type of library called a Partitioned Data Set Extended (PDSE). This type of library is good for large data sets such as production PROCLIB.

KEYLEN—Specifies length of key in bytes for VSAM

KEYOFF—Gives the offset for the key of a key-sequenced VSAM data set. With SMS, VSAM data sets can be allocated within the JCL.

LIKE—Copies data set attributes.

MGMTCLAS—Supplies management class data set attributes for migration and backup.

RECORG—Indicates type of VSAM data set being created.

REFDD—Copies JCL attributes for the data set.

SECMODEL—Copies JCL attributes for the data set.

☞ Suggest:

- Using AVGREC for space allocation.

- Allocating PDSEs for large libraries (DSN-TYPE=LIBRARY).

- Not coding UNIT for DASD if UNIT is not needed.

- Letting system select storage class and management class instead of coding these in the JCL.

3.1. SMS—AVGREC FORMAT

```
//ddname2  DD  DSN=data.set.name,
//             DISP=(begin,normal-step,abend-step),
//             UNIT=unitname,
//             SPACE=(lrecl,(primary,secondary,),RLSE),
//             AVGREC=type,
//             RECFM=xx,LRECL=##
```

- Lrecl|avglrecl—Provides SPACE for AVGREC using record length. Use LRECL size for fixed block data sets; average LRECL size for variable block data sets.

- AVGREC—Provides SPACE in number of records.

- Type—Provides increment for number of records.

  - U—asks for records in units.

  - K—asks for records in increments of 1,024.

  - M—asks for records in increments of 1,048,576.

SMS—AVGREC Parameter

- Space requirement is calculated by number of records. This gives device independence and user does not have to figure out how many records fit in a block, how many blocks fit on a track to calculate SPACE.

- primary—100 x 1024 = 102,400 records +

- secondary—10 x 1024 x 15 extents = 153,600 records.

- Primary at 102,400 + secondary at 153,600 gives a total of 256,000 records.

- Space is allocated and released in tracks (the smallest a data set can be is 1 track).

  See: *When to Code DD Parameters (i.e., using tape, do not code space).*

  See: *ESA Space Allocation.*

SMS—AVGREC—Create Data Set Example

```
//MSTRO     DD  DSN=ABCP.GMSTR(+1),
//              DISP=(NEW,CATLG,DELETE),
//              UNIT=SYSDA,
//              SPACE=(80,(100,10),RLSE),      *SMS DASD
//              AVGREC=K,                      *SMS DASD
//              RECFM=FB,LRECL=80
```

- With SMS, UNIT might not need to be coded.

- First subparameter of SPACE "80" gives average record length as opposed to tracks, cylinders, or block size.

- AVGREC=K—Asks for space in thousands of records.

- With operating system release MVS/ESA 4.1 and higher the system can calculate the block size.

3.2. DATACLAS FORMAT

```
//DATACLAS=name
```

- Name—Gives the site-specific data class name up to 8 characters. Name is defined by the storage administrator, and can be automatically assigned via ACS routines. Data class can contain values for: AVGREC|SPACE, KEYLEN—direct data sets, LRECL, RECFM, RETPD/EXPDT, VOL—volume count, VSAM-CISIZE, FREESPACE, IMBED, KEYOFF, RECORG, REPLICATE, SHAREOPTIONS.

DATACLAS Example

```
//WORKOUT   DD  DSN=PAP.WRK.TRANS,
//              DISP=(NEW,CATLG,DELETE),
//              DATACLAS=DCLS010,
//              RECFM=FB,LRECL=150
```

- Keywords coded in JCL override DATACLAS values. See ISMF panel off TSO/ISPF to view values for data classes at your site.

- Data class is often used for standard data sets (e.g., libraries).

3.3. DSNTYPE FORMAT

```
//              DSNTYPE=LIBRARY
```

- LIBRARY—Specifies a Partitioned Data Set Extended (PDSE). A PDSE must be SMS managed; has up to 123 extents; never needs to be compressed; does not need directory space; has faster access; and can now contain load modules.

DSNTYPE Example

```
//DDOUT    DD  DSN=PXX.COB.LOADLIB,
//              DISP=(NEW,CATLG,DELETE),
//              DATACLAS=DCCOBOL,
//              DSNTYPE=LIBRARY
```

- DSNTYPE=LIBRARY specifies a PDSE.

3.4. KEYLEN FORMAT

```
//              keylen=##
```

- Specifies length of key in bytes.

- ##—is the number of bytes for the key.

3.5. KEYOFF FORMAT

```
//              KEYOFF=##
```

- Defines a key-sequenced VSAM data set.

- ##—is number of bytes, offset of 1ST byte is 0.

KEYOFF Example

```
//DDOUT    DD  DSN=PXX.VSM.MASTER,
//              DISP=(NEW,CATLG,DELETE),
//              DATACLAS=DCVSAMO,
//              RECORG=KS,
//              KEYOFF=9
//              KEYLEN=9
```

- First byte of key is in the 10th position of each record. KEYLEN— the key is 9 bytes long. Storage class and group are assigned via ACS routines.

3.6. LIKE FORMAT

```
//              LIKE=data.set.name
```

* Copies data set attributes—AVGREC|SPACE, DSNTYPE, KEYLEN|KEYOFF if VSAM, LRECL, RECFM|RECORG if VSAM). LIKE overrides data class.

LIKE Example

```
//DDOUT    DD  DSN=PXX.LIB.COBLIB,
//              DISP=(NEW,CATLG,DELETE),
//              LIKE=PXX.MODEL.COBLIB
```

* Copies PXX.LIB.COBLIB attributes from cataloged model data set PXX.MODEL.COBLIB.

3.7. MGMTCLAS FORMAT

```
//              MGMTCLAS=name
```

* Name—Gives management class name up to 8 characters. The name is defined by storage administrator and can be automatically assigned via ACS routines. Defines data set attributes for migration and backup. Limits GDSs on DASD, releases unused space, automatically restores archived data.

* EXPDT/RETPD coded in JCL—Does not override management class retention.

MGMTCLAS Example

```
//WORKOUT   DD  DSN=PAP.WRK.TRANS,
//              DISP=(NEW,CATLG,DELETE),
//              DATACLAS=DCLS010,
//              MGMTCLAS=MCWORK
```

* Example is unusual since storage class and management class are usually assigned via ACS routines coded by the storage administrator.

3.8. RECORG FORMAT

```
//                    RECORG=KS|ES|RR|LS
```

RECORG can be one of the following:

1) KS—Indicates key sequenced.

2) ES—Indicates entry sequenced.

3) RR—Indicates relative record.

4) LS—Indicates linear space (data only, VSAM cluster contains no control information).

- Example below creates an SMS-managed VSAM data set with JCL instead of using the IBM utility IDCAMS to delete, define, and copy data to the VSAM data set.

- KS—Indicates key-sequenced data set.

- KEYOFF—First byte of key is in position 10.

- KEYLEN—Specifies length of key in bytes (9 bytes).

RECORG Example

```
//DDOUT      DD   DSN=PXX.VSM.MASTER,
//                DISP=(NEW,CATLG,DELETE),
//                DATACLAS=DCVSAMO,
//                RECORG=KS,
//                KEYOFF=9,
//                KEYLEN=9
```

3.9. REFDD FORMAT

```
//                  REFDD=*.stepname.ddname
```

- Copies JCL attributes—such as AVGREC, SPACE, DSNTYPE, KEYLEN, KEYOFF, LRECL, RECFM and RECORG from DD statement.

  ☞ Suggest not using, as step cannot be restarted; code the JCL parameters instead.

  ✍ *See: Refer Back.*

- System uses parameters on DD statement containing:

  1) REFDD.

  2) Referred to by REFDD.

  3) Parameters from data class of referred to DD.

REFDD Example

```
//STEP05    EXEC PGM=pgmname ...
//DDOT      DD  DSN=PXX.WRK.TRANS,
//              DISP=(NEW,CATLG,DELETE),
//              SPACE=(CYL,(10,1),RLSE),
//              UNIT=SYSDA,
//              DCB=(RECFM=FB,LRECL=80)
//STEP10    EXEC PGM=pgmname ...
//DDOT2     DD  DSN=PXX.WRK.TRANS2,
//              DISP=(NEW,CATLG,DELETE),
//              UNIT=SYSDA,
//              REFDD=*.STEP05.DDOT
```

- PXX.WRK.TRANS2 copies JCL attributes from PXX.WRK.TRANS in STEP05.

3.10. SECMODEL FORMAT

```
//              SECMODEL=(profile) or (profile.GENERIC)
```

- Assigns RACF protection to non-temporary data sets. Usually the security administrator handles this automatically through RACF or similar security software.

SECMODEL Example

```
//WORKOUT  DD  DSN=PAP.WRK.TRANS,
//              SECMODEL=(profile),
//              DISP=(NEW,CATLG,DELETE),
//              DATACLAS=DCLS010
```

3.11. STORCLAS FORMAT

```
//              STORCLAS=name
```

- Name—Gives storage class name up to 8 characters that is defined by storage administrator. Normally storage class is automatically assigned via ACS routines and is not coded in JCL. Defines data set attributes for service level (performance), where SMS stores the data set and controls dual copy.

STORCLAS Example

```
//WORKOUT  DD  DSN=PAP.WRK.TRANS,
//              DISP=(NEW,CATLG,DELETE),
//              DATACLAS=DCLS010,
//              STORCLAS=SCWORK
```

- Shows management class is assigned via ACS routines. Normally storage class is also assigned via ACS routines and not coded in JCL.

3.12. SMS—UNIT PARAMETER— MIGHT NOT BE NEEDED

• UNIT—Assigns a device, either tape or DASD. With SMS, UNIT might not be needed when writing to DASD or might be ignored.

• When coding SMS JCL keyword DATACLAS, DSN and DISP only might need to be coded because in some shops SPACE and UNIT are provided via the data class. Data class could automatically be assigned as a result of ACS routines. Parameters coded in the user's JCL override DATACLAS values.

See: DATACLAS.

3.13. SMS RULES

- SMS DASD data sets are cataloged at the beginning of the step, not at the end of the job step.

  ☞ IMPORTANT: This means user no longer receives a NOT CATLGD2 message for SMS managed data sets. Instead user receives a data set already exists JCL error.

- All SMS data sets are cataloged. For instance, if NEW,KEEP is coded when creating a (+1) GDS, the data set is still cataloged by G000#V00, but it is not <u>rolled-in</u> to the GDG base (which means the generation cannot be accessed by coding a +0).

  See: GDS Roll-In States.

- Do not code STEPCAT or JOBCAT if SMS is active.

- If SMS keywords are used in JCL, and SMS is not active, they are checked for syntax and ignored. This is the rule, except when creating a VSAM data set via JCL, in which case the system creates the data set but it is not a VSAM data set.

- Keywords are valid when creating data sets on DASD.

- Data set naming can be used as a criterion to automatically assign the classes via ACS routines:

  1) Management class.

  2) Storage class.

  3) Data class.

- Good data set naming conventions should indicate the type of data set and its use (e.g., VSAM; GDG; work; library; online or batch; critical or standard; high or regular performance, or duplex or not duplex).

- The shop's storage administrator writes ACS routines in a CLIST-type language.

3.14. SMS OVERRIDES

Data Class

*   JCL Keywords (i.e., AVGREC, SPACE, KEYLEN, KEYOFF, LRECL, RECORG/RECFM, RETPD/EXPDT, vol count of VOLUME) override the ACS Data Class routines.

*   ACS Data Class routines override the JCL Parameter DATACLAS.

Management Class

*   ACS Management Class routines override the JCL Parameter MGMTCLAS. Management Class overrides the JCL Keywords EXPDT, or RETPD.

LIKE Parameter

*   JCL Keywords (i.e., AVGREC, SPACE, KEYLEN, KEYOFF, LRECL, RECORG, RECFM) override the JCL Parameter LIKE.

Storage Class

*   ACS Storage Class routines override the JCL Parameter STORCLAS. The JCL Parameter STORCLAS overrides JCL Keywords (i.e., UNIT, VOL=SER).

*   Storage Administrator can set up a special storage class that specifies GUARANTEED SPACE=YES, then the JCL Keyword VOL=SER overrides SMS. This is done by exception and few people have authority to use it (i.e., Database Administrator).

Ways to Code and Use JCL **4**

4.1. WHEN TO CODE DD PARAMETERS*

	Input Cataloged		Input Not Cataloged		Output	
Parameter	DASD	Tape	DASD	Tape	DASD	Tape
DSN	X	X	X	X	X	X

- Input: Exceptions, include for non-labeled tape, and when coding BLP for tape.

- Output: Exceptions, work data sets used in 1 job step (i.e., sort works).

DSN Example—Code Data Set Name

```
//DDIN      DD   DSN=ABC.SIMPLE,
//               DISP=(SHR,KEEP,KEEP)
```

&↻ **See:** Data Set Name.

DSN Example—Do not code Data Set Name

```
//SORTWK01 DD   UNIT=SYSDA,
//               SPACE=(CYL,(50,5))
```

* X -- Code parameter, O -- Code parameter under conditions specified.

	Input Cataloged		Input Not Cataloged		Output	
Parameter	DASD	Tape	DASD	Tape	DASD	Tape
DISP	X	X	X	X	X	X

- Output: Exceptions, work data sets used in 1 job step (i.e., sort works; see default below).

DISP Examples

Create—Use in 1 step. Default if DISP is not coded:

```
//              DISP=(NEW,DELETE,DELETE)
```

Create simple or GDG data sets:

```
//              DISP=(NEW,CATLG,DELETE)
```

SMS—Create VSAM in JCL:

```
//              DISP=(NEW,CATLG,DELETE)
```

- VSAM data set is normally created using IDCAMS.

  See: IDCAMS.

Library data set and 99% of the time for VSAM use:

```
//              DISP=SHR
```

- When SHR is coded the default is KEEP,KEEP.

- Code for simple or GDG when multiple users are permitted.

Exclusive use, i.e., updating a GDG use:

```
//              DISP=(OLD,KEEP,KEEP)
```

Simple data set—Last time used and not accessed by any other job use:

```
//              DISP=(OLD,DELETE,KEEP)
```

Simple data set—Accessed by another job:

```
//              DISP=(OLD,KEEP,KEEP)
```

  See: Data Set Names.

Parameter	Input Cataloged		Input Not Cataloged		Output	
	DASD	Tape	DASD	Tape	DASD	Tape
UNIT			X	X	X	X

- SMS Output—UNIT might not be needed for DASD output or might be ignored.

    &⁄ *See:* Standards.

UNIT=AFF		X				

- Input—Use to concatenate tapes.

    &⁄ *See:* Tape Concatenation (UNIT=AFF).

UNIT=DEFER		X		X		X

- Tape—Specifies don't mount until opened by program.

UNIT Examples

```
//          UNIT=SYSDA
```

- Asks for a generic DASD unit per shop standards.

```
//          UNIT=AFF=SYSUT1
```

- For tape concatenation use same unit specified on ddname SYSUT1.

```
//          UNIT=(CART,,DEFER)
```

- Asks for tape mount but do not request until data set is opened by the program.

Parameter	Input Cataloged		Input Not Cataloged		Output	
	DASD	Tape	DASD	Tape	DASD	Tape
VOL=SER=nnnnnn			X	X	Avoid	

- SMS Output—Do not code if shop is using SMS. If coded, could be ignored in an SMS environment.

VOL=(,,,99)						X

- Output—Writing to more than 5 tape volumes.

VOL=(,RETAIN)	X		X		X	

- Tape—Use if data set is accessed in another step in the job. Don't code the last time data set is accessed, because tape doesn't unload—useless on multi-reel data sets.

VOL Examples

```
//            VOL=SER=001234
```

- Asks for a specific volume, an input tape from outside that is not cataloged to the system.

```
//            VOL=SER=(123456,987654)
```

- Shows a multiple volume request.

```
//            VOL=(,,,99)
```

- Writes to more than 5 volumes.

```
//            UNIT=CART,
//            VOL=(,RETAIN)
```

- Asks for the tape volume to remain mounted.

Parameter	Input Cataloged		Input Not Cataloged		Output	
	DASD	Tape	DASD	Tape	DASD	Tape
SPACE					X	

- Output—Space is required to allocate DASD data sets. With SMS, space can be provided if system automatically assigns a data class that provides space.

Examples

```
//          SPACE=(CYL,(10,1),RLSE)
```

- Asks for space in cylinders. Gives 10 primary cylinders, 1 secondary cylinder. Gives the secondary amount 15 times. RLSE—releases unused cylinders.

```
//          SPACE=(TRK,(150,15),RLSE)
```

- Asks for space in tracks. Gives 150 primary tracks, 15 secondary tracks. Gives the secondary amount 15 times. RLSE—releases unused tracks.

```
//          SPACE=(23440,(300,30),RLSE)
```

- Asks for space in blocks. Gives 300 primary blocks of 23440, 30 secondary blocks. Gives the secondary amount 15 times. (2 blocks fit on a track.) RLSE—releases unused tracks.

```
//          AVGREC=K,      *SMS AVGREC
//          SPACE=(80,(10,1),RLSE)
```

- Uses SMS to request space in number of records. 80 is the logical record length, 10,000 primary records 1,000 secondary records. Gives the secondary amount 15 times. RLSE—releases unused tracks.

Parameter	Input Cataloged		Input Not Cataloged		Output	
	DASD	Tape	DASD	Tape	DASD	Tape
LABEL		X		X		X

- Code if tape label is:
  1) Not the first label on the tape.
  2) Not a standard (BLP, NSL, NL).
  3) When creating output to specify retention.
  4) When reading a foreign tape (i.e. not defined to CA-1)

Examples

```
//          LABEL=(3,SL)        *DEFAULT (1,SL)
```
- Asks for third label on the tape.

```
//          LABEL=(,NL)         *DEFAULT (1,SL)
```
- Asks for non-labeled tape.

```
//          LABEL=(,BLP)        *NO SECURITY
```
- Bypasses label processing and security.

```
//          LABEL=EXPDT=99000 *CA-1
```
- Indicates tape retention for CA-1—keep as long as cataloged to OS/390.

ESA Example

```
//              EXPDT=98000        *LABEL NOT NEEDED
```

- Value 98000 indicates a foreign tape to CA-1.

Example 1—Creating Tape Output (Older Coding Technique)

```
//MSTRO     DD  DSN=ABCP.GMSTR(+1),
//              DISP=(NEW,CATLG,DELETE),
//              UNIT=CART,
//              LABEL=EXPDT=99000,
//              DCB=(P.MODL,RECFM=FB,LRECL=80,BLKSIZE=32720)
```

- Writes data set to tape. With older coding the keywords LABEL and DCB are needed, block size must be coded, and P.MODL is needed without SMS. Compare to example below.

Example 2—Using Newer Techniques with ESA and SMS

```
//MSTRO     DD  ...
//              EXPDT=99000
//              RECFM=FB,LRECL=80
```

	Input Cataloged		Input Not Cataloged		Output	
Parameter	DASD	Tape	DASD	Tape	DASD	Tape
DCB		X		X	X	X

- Input—Required for non-labeled tape or when reading a tape using BLP.

  ☞ Suggest BLP should be coded by exception. Also user can request BLP and system might override and mount the tape SL. Some shops only have one initiator set up to allow BLP.

- Output—Always code.

- ESA Output—Don't code block size.

- ESA—DCB keyword is not needed.

DCB Example—Older coding

```
//            DCB=(RECFM=FB,LRECL=80,BLKSIZE=6160)
```

DCB Example—ESA

```
//            RECFM=FB,LRECL=80,BLKSIZE=0
//            RECFM=FB,LRECL=80
```

DCB=model.data set					X	X

- Output—Code as first subparameter of DCB when creating a (+1) GDS.

Model DSCB Example—Older coding

```
//            DCB=(PMOD.DSCB,RECFM=FB,LRECL=80)
```

SMS Example—Model DSCB not needed

```
//            RECFM=FB,LRECL=80
```

- ESA block size and DCB are not needed.

	Input Cataloged		Input Not Cataloged		Output	
Parameter	DASD	Tape	DASD	Tape	DASD	Tape
DEN		X		X		X

- Tape: Dual density drive, default-highest, must specify for lower density. Specify DEN=4 for 6250, DEN=3 for 1600, DEN=2 for 800 BPI (Bits Per Inch).

DEN Example

```
//              DCB=DEN=4        * 6250 BPI
```

ESA Example—DCB is not needed

```
//              DEN=4            * DCB NOT NEEDED
```

Parameter	Input Cataloged		Input Not Cataloged		Output	
	DASD	Tape	DASD	Tape	DASD	Tape
BUFNO	X	X	X	X	X	X

- Use when performing I/O for large sequential data sets to reduce run time. Default is usually 5, max is 255. Coding additional buffers for large data sets can significantly reduce run time. User might need to increase REGION parameter. Do not code a BUFNO value at less than 5.

Physical Sequential—Example

```
//          DCB=BUFNO=10
```

ESA Example

```
//          BUFNO=10
```

BUFNI	X				X	

- Accessing large VSAM data set via key and job is running too long. Default is 2 data and 1-index buffers.

Example

```
//          AMP=('BUFNI=11,BUFND=2')
```

BUFND	X	X		X	X	

- Accessing a large VSAM data set sequentially and job is running too long. Default 2 data and 1-index buffers.

Example

```
//          AMP=('BUFNI=1,BUFND=23')
```

Parameter	Input Cataloged		Input Not Cataloged		Output	
	DASD	Tape	DASD	Tape	DASD	Tape
FREE	X	X			X	X

- Deallocates resource when closed instead of at end of step which is the default—FREE=END. If step abends after data set is closed, system already processed data set using normal DISP instead of ABEND.

Example

```
//REPTOT    DD   SYSOUT=A,
//               FREE=CLOSE
```

4.2. COND COMPARE WITH IF . . . ENDIF

TRUE step does not run.   TRUE step RUNS!

```
//          COND=(#,oper)      //          IF  (RC oper  #)  THEN...
```

XX-MNEMONIC			XX-MNEMONIC OR CHARACTER		
EQ	EQual		EQ	Equal	=
GT	Greater Than		GT	Greater Than	>
GE	Greater or Equal		GE	Greater or Equal	>=
LT	Less Than		LT	Less Than	<
LE	Less or Equal		LE	Less or Equal	<=
NE	Not Equal		NE	Not Equal	¬=
--			AND	logical AND	&
--			NOT	logical NOT	¬
--			OR	logical OR	|

- Mnemonic—Code blank before and after.

- Character—Blanks not needed.

- Code one way for consistency; the mnemonic is easier to read.

- Avoid using NOT, as it is very confusing.

4.2.1. Return Code Table—Understand COND and IF Logic

* COND runs if result is false. See tables below with explanations.

* IF statement step runs when result is true.

RC	oper	Previous Step(s)	Result	Runs	RC	oper	Previous Step(s)	Result	Runs
1	LE	0	False	Yes	0	LE	0	True	Yes
1	LE	1	True	No	1	LE	0	False	No

```
//          COND=(1,LE)     //          IF (RC LE 0) THEN ...
```

* COND—Is 1 less than or equal to 0? Answer is false so step runs.

* COND—Is 1 less than or equal to 1? Answer is true so step does not run.

RC	oper	Previous Step(s)	Result	Runs	RC	oper	Previous Step(s)	Result	Runs
0	LT	0	False	Yes	0	LT	1	True	Yes
0	LT	1	True	No	1	LT	1	False	No

```
//          COND=(0,LT)     //          IF (RC LT 1) THEN ...
```

* COND—Is 0 less than 0? Answer if false so step runs.

* COND—Is 0 less than 1? Answer is true so step does not run.

RC	oper	Previous Step(s)	Result	Runs	RC	oper	Previous Step(s)	Result	Runs
1	NE	0	False	Yes	0	NE	0	True	Yes
1	NE	1	True	No	1	NE	0	False	No

```
//          COND=(0,NE)     //          IF (RC EQ 0) THEN ...
```

* COND—Is 0 not equal to 0? Answer is false so step runs.

* COND—Is 0 not equal to 1? Answer is true so step does not run.

4.2.2. Convert COND to IF

Convert COND Parameters to IF Expressions

If LE subtract 1 from number:

COND=(5,LE) 5 - 1 = 4, result: (RC LE 4)

If LT add 1 to number:

COND=(4,LT) 4 + 1 = 5, result: (RC LT 5)

If GT subtract 1 from number:

COND=(5,GT) 5 - 1 = 4, result: (RC GT 4)

If GE add 1 to number:

COND=(4,GE) 4 + 1 = 5, result: (RC GE 5)

Example 1: 0 Return Code Is Good

```
       COND                              IF
//          COND=(1,LE)     //          IF (RC LE 0) THEN...
//          COND=(0,LT)     //          IF (RC LT 1) THEN...
//          COND=(0,NE)     //          IF (RC EQ 0) THEN...
```

Example 2: 0-4 Return Code Is Good

```
//          COND=(5,LE)     //          IF (RC LE 4) THEN...
//          COND=(4,LT)     //          IF (RC LT 5) THEN...
```

Example 3: Execute Only If Previous Step Abended

```
//          COND=(ONLY)     //          IF (ABEND) THEN...
```

Example 4: COND & IF ... ENDIF

```
//S2        EXEC PGM=ABC           //S2        EXEC PGM=ABC
//* *   *   * * * *                //* *   *   * * *
//* SORT                           //* SORT
//* *   *   * * * *                //* *   *   * * *
//S4        EXEC PGM=SORT,         //          IF (RC LE 0) THEN
//              COND=(1,LE)        //S4        EXEC PGM=SORT
//ddname   DD ...                  //ddname   DD ...
//*                                //         ENDIF
//* *   *   * * * *                //* *   *   * * *
//* ABEND                          //* PRINT
//* *   *   * * * *                //* *   *   * * *
//S6        EXEC PGM=ABEND,        //          IF (RC LE 4) THEN
//              COND=(5,GT,S4)     //S6        EXEC PGM=PRINT
//*                                //         ELSE
//* *   *   * * * *                //* *   *   * * *
//* PRINT                          //* ABEND
//* *   *   * * * *                //* *   *   * * *
//S8        EXEC PGM=PRINT,        //S8        EXEC PGM=ABEND
//              COND=(5,LE)        //* RUNS IF S6 DOES NOT
//**                               //         ENDIF
```

Example 2: Abend and Print Steps

```
//S4          EXEC.PGM=SORT        //S4          EXEC PGM=SORT
...                                ...
//*  *  *  *  *  *  *              //*  *  *  *  *  *
//* ABEND                          //* ABEND
//*  *  *  *  *  *  *              //*  *  *  *  *  *
//S6          EXEC PGM=ABEND,      //           IF  (S4.RC GT 4)THEN
//               COND=(5,GT,S4)    //S6          EXEC PGM=ABEND
//*                                //           ENDIF
//*  *  *  *  *  *  *              //*  *  *  *  *  *
//* PRINT                          //* PRINT
//*  *  *  *  *  *  *              //*  *  *  *  *  *
//S8          EXEC PGM=PRINT,      //           IF  (RC LE 4) THEN
//               COND=(5,LE)       //S8          EXEC PGM=PRINT
...                                ...
//**                               //           ENDIF
```

- User can insert an ABEND step to facilitate job restart. Code abend step after programs that get a bad return code, but do not ABEND (i.e., SORT, IDCAMS, IBM Utilities).

Step-Specific: RUN = FALSE for Step Restart

```
//           IF  (S2.RC = 0) OR  (S2.RUN = FALSE)  THEN
...
//               ENDIF
```

- With COND specific step checks system allowed restart. With IF specific step checks user must code or (step#.RUN=FALSE) for system to allow step restart.

4.3. THREE WAYS TO CODE JCL

- The 3 ways to code JCL are:

  1) Cataloged Procedure (PROC)

  2) Plain JCL

  3) In-Stream Procedure

4.3.1. Cataloged Procedure (PROC)

- A cataloged procedure consists of JCL coded in two different libraries and control statements in a third library, usually called PARMLIB.

- JCL created in the JCLLIB library calls the cataloged procedure to run from the PROCLIB library. PROCs found in PROCLIB contain PROC, EXEC PGM, and DD statements as needed. See below.

- Control statements (e.g., SORT, IDCAMS) must be coded in a member in a separate PARMLIB library.

PROC Format

```
//procname PROC
//* * * * * * * * * * * * * * * *
//* COMMENTS
//* * * * * * * * * * * * * * * *
//procstep EXEC  PGM=pgmname
//ddname    DD    DSN=dataset.name,
//                DISP=…
//ddname    DD    SYSOUT=x
//SYSIN     DD    DSN=xxxx.PARMLIB(member),
//                DISP=SHR
```

- PROC Statement—This label indicates beginning of PROC.

- //*—Comment statements contain internal documentation.

- EXEC PGM—Tells system what load module to run.

- DDs—Define the input and output data sets required to successfully run the program.

- SYSIN—Shows an example of control statements being read from a library.

- //—Indicates end of JCL and is not coded in a PROC.

JCL That Calls the PROC to Run

- JCL found in JCLLIB contains the JOB and EXEC PROC statements. It can also contain JES2 statements, a JOBLIB statement, and a JCLLIB statement, along with DD OVERRIDES that are coded as needed. See sample JCLLIB contents below.

- Control statements (e.g., SORT, IDCAMS) can be coded in-stream as an override.

JCL Format

```
//jobname   JOB  (acct),'pgm-name',
//               CLASS=x,
//               MSGCLASS=x
/*keyword   parameter,parameter     *JES2 IF NEEDED
//JOBLIB    DD  DSN=library,         *LIST LOADLIBS
//               DISP=SHR
//          DD  DSN=library2,
//               DISP=SHR
//               JCLLIB ORDER=(library1,library2)
//jobstep   EXEC PROC=procname
//procstep.ddname   DD   parameter    *IF NEEDED
//procstep.SYSIN    DD   *            *IF NEEDED
      control statements
/*
//
```

- JOB—Indicates beginning of a batch job.
- /*keyword—JES2 control statement is coded if needed.
- JOBLIB—Lists the libraries where system should search for application load modules.
- JCLLIB—Tells the system where to find the cataloged procedures ESA and higher releases.
- EXEC PROC—Tells system what member to execute in PROCLIB. In OS/390 EXEC name without the PROC keyword defaults to execute a PROC.
- Procstep.ddname—Allows user to override parameters on the DD statement.
- Procstep.SYSIN—Shows an example to override control statements in a PROC.
- /*—Indicates end of control statements
- //—Indicates end of JCL.

4.3.2. "Plain JCL"

- This is JCL created in a single library that is not destined for production. This JCL might be a utility used to print test data sets. This JCL contains JOB, EXEC PGM, and DD statements as needed. See below:

- Control statements (e.g., SORT, IDCAMS) can be coded in-stream.

"Plain JCL" Format

```
//jobname   JOB (acct),'pgm-name',
//               CLASS=x,
//               MSGCLASS=x
/*keyword   parameter,parameter    *JES2 IF NEEDED
//JOBLIB    DD  DSN=library,        *LIST LOADLIBS
//              DISP=SHR
//          DD  DSN=library2,
//              DISP=SHR
//* COMMENTS
//stepname EXEC PGM=pgmname
//ddname    DD  DSN=dataset.name,
//              DISP= ...
//ddname    DD  SYSOUT=x
//SYSIN     DD  *
    control statements
/*
//
```

- JOB—Indicates beginning of a batch job.

- /*keyword—JES2 control statement is coded if needed.

- JOBLIB—Lists the libraries where system should search for application load modules.

- EXEC PGM—Tells system what load module to run.

- DDs—Defines the input and output data sets required to successfully run the program.

- SYSIN—Shows an example of control statements being read in plain JCL.

- /*—Indicates end of control statements.

- //—Indicates end of JCL.

4.3.3. In-Stream Procedure

* JCL created in a single library (logonid.JCL.CNTL library). Software vendors sometimes code their JCL using this method. This JCL contains the following statements: JOB, PROC, EXEC PGM, DDs, PEND, and EXEC PROC, along with DD overrides if needed. See below:

  ☞ Suggest that user not use in-stream procedure, as these are difficult to maintain and run.

In-Stream Procedure Format

```
//logon1    JOB (acct),'pgm-name',
//          CLASS=x,
//          NOTIFY=logon,
//          MSGCLASS=x
//*JES2 control statement(s)
//JOBLIB    DD  DSN=library,
//          DISP=SHR
//* COMMENTS
//procname PROC
//* COMMENTS
//procstep EXEC PGM=pgmname
//ddname    DD  DSN=dataset.name,
//          DISP=. . .
//ddname    DD  SYSOUT=x
//SYSIN     DD  DSN=xxxx.PARMLIB(member),
//          DISP=SHR
//          PEND
//jobstep  EXEC PROC=procname
//procstep.ddname DD parameter   *DD OVERRIDE
//
```

* JOB—Indicates beginning of a batch job.

* /*keyword—JES2 control statement is coded if needed.

* JOBLIB—Lists the libraries where system should search for application load modules.

* PROC—Indicates beginning of PROC.

* EXEC PGM—Tells system what load module to run.

* DDs—Define the input and output data sets required to successfully run the program.

- SYSIN—Shows an example of control statements being read from a library.

- PEND—Indicates end of PROC.

- EXEC PROC—Tells system what member to execute in PROCLIB.

- Procstep.ddname—Allows user to override parameters on the DD statement.

- Procstep.SYSIN—Shows an example to override control statements in a PROC.

- /*—Indicates end of control statements

- //—Indicates end of JCL.

4.4. PROCEDURE OVERRIDES (CATALOGED OR IN-STREAM)

Overrides are coded in the JCLLIB library (library that contains the JOB and EXEC PROC statements) to allow a user to easily change parameters, or add a DD statement to a PROC. There are 3 types of overrides:

1) DD Overrides

2) EXEC PGM Overrides

3) Symbolic Overrides

4.4.1. DD Override

- The DD Override allows a one-time change to a PROC.

- Format for a DD override is procstep.ddname. Procstep is found in columns 3-10 of the EXEC PGM statement; DD name is found in columns 3-10 of the DD statement in the PROC.

- Code only the parameters that are changing.

- Users can add a DD statement to a PROC using overrides. System places the statement last in the step. Overrides must be coded in order, except in ESA.

  See: DD Override Order.

DD Override Format

```
//jobname   JOB...
//jobstep   EXEC PROC=procname
//procstep.ddname DD parameter(s)
```

PROC Being Overridden Example

```
//ABCPROC      PROC
//PS010     EXEC PGM=ABCPGM
//MASTIN    DD   DSN=ABCP.VMAST,
//               DISP=SHR
//MASTOT    DD   DSN=ABCP.WRK,
//               DISP=(NEW,CATLG,DELETE),
//               SPACE=(CYL,(10,1),RLSE),
//               RECFM=FB,LRECL=80,BLKSIZE=0
```

DD Override Examples

DISP Is Read from PROC Example 1

```
//STEP01   EXEC PROC=ABCPROC
//PS010.MASTIN DD DSN=ABCT.VMAST
```

• When comma is not coded, parameters are used from the PROC.

DISP Is Coded as Override Example 2

```
//STEP01   EXEC PROC=ABCPROC
//PS010.MASTIN DD DSN=ABCT.VMAST,
//              DISP=SHR
```

• When comma is coded, user must code the parameters that follow.

SPACE Override Example 3

```
//STEP01   EXEC PROC=ABCPROC
//PS010.MASTOT DD SPACE=(CYL,(20,2),RLSE)
```

• Asks for twice the amount of space coded in the PROC.

4.4.2. EXEC PGM Override

- The program name cannot be changed but other parameters on the EXEC PGM statement can be changed.

EXEC PGM Override Format

```
//jobstep   EXEC PROC=procname,
//                parameter.procstep=new-value
```

PROC Being Overridden Example

```
//ABCPROC      PROC
//PS010     EXEC PGM=ABCPGM
...
```

EXEC PGM Override Examples

Changes Time in a Specific Step Example 1

```
//STEP01    EXEC PROC=ABCPROC,
//                TIME.PS010=(4,30)
```

Changes Time in Every Step Example 2

```
//STEP01    EXEC PROC=ABCPROC,
//                TIME=(4,30)
```

Nullifies Time in Every Step Example 3

```
//STEP01    EXEC PROC=ABCPROC,
//                TIME=
```

4.4.3. Symbolic Override

- Symbolic overrides change values coded in PROC and are assigned when the job runs.

- The value must be enclosed in apostrophes if it contains special characters.

```
//jobstep  EXEC PROC=procname,
//              symbolic='value'[,
//              symbolic2='value2'] …
```

Symbolic Override Example

```
//ABCD100   JOB (ABC,010),'PRINT INVENTORY',
//              CLASS=A,
//              MSGCLASS=S
//JS001     EXEC PROC=ABCPROC,
//              LIB='TEST',    *SYMBOLIC OVERRIDE
//              DSN='ABCT'     *SYMBOLIC OVERRIDE
//
```

PROC being overriden Example

```
//ABCPROC  PROC LIB='PROD',   *DEFAULT VALUE
//              DSN=ABCP       *DEFAULT VALUE
//PS010    EXEC PGM=pgmname
//STEPLIB  DD   DSN=&LIB..LOADLIB,
//              DISP=SHR
//DDIN     DD   DSN=&DSN..DATA,
//              DISP=SHR
```

- When PROC runs MVS substitutes: TEST.LOADLIB, and ABCT.DATA using the symbolic overrides.

4.5. SYMBOLIC

- Symbolics are a method of changing values in a PROC.

  &✐ See: Three Ways to Code JCL.

- Code a symbolic for values that change going from test to production such as data set name. Exception: if coded using SET, then a symbolic can be used in "Plain JCL" too.

  &✐ See: SET.

- Symbolic begins with an & and must end with a period if the following special characters do not immediately follow the symbolic:

  , ' *) / - + =

- Period separates symbolic from the rest of the JCL code.

- Symbolic name can be up to 7 characters. See symbolic name V4.1 (ESA allows up to 8 characters)

Formats

```
&symbolic.   or   &symbolic
```

Example

```
//STEPLIB  DD  DSN=&LIB..LOADLIB,
//             DISP=SHR
```

PROC Symbolic Default

- PROC Symbolic Default means the symbolic is given a value
on the PROC label statement in the PROC. Values coded here
are overridden by values coded in JCLLIB on the EXEC PROC
statement. 'Value' is assigned when the PROC runs.

  See: Procedure Override.

Symbolic Format

```
//procname PROC symbolic='value',
//              symbolic2='value2'
   ...
```

Symbolic Example

```
//jobname  JOB ...
//jobstep  EXEC PROC=procname
//


//procname PROC LIB='PROD'
//stepname EXEC PGM=pgmname
//STEPLIB  DD  DSN=&LIB..LOADLIB,
//             DISP=SHR
   ...
```

- When PROC runs, MVS substitutes: PROD.LOADLIB

  Suggest that user not overuse the symbolic.

  See: Symbolic Override.

4.6. DD BACKWARD REFERENCES (REFER-BACKS)

• The DD backward reference copies information from a previous statement within the job. Parameters that can be a backward reference include: DSN, DCB, EXEC PGM, and VOL.

☞ Suggest not coding these, because when they point back to another step, user cannot step restart. Just code the parameters you need. When user codes the parameters instead of coding a refer-back JCL is easier to update.

✐ See: Tape File Stacking for a practical VOL=REF Example.

DCB Refer Back Same Step Format 1

• System copies DCB information from the data set listed.

```
//              DCB=dataset.name
```

DCB Refer Back Same Step Example 1

```
//DDIN1    DD  DSN=ABC.SIMPLE,
//              DISP=SHR
...
//DDOT2    DD  DSN=ABC.SIMPLE2,
//              DISP=(NEW,CATLG,DELETE),
//              UNIT=CART,
//              DCB=ABC.SIMPLE
```

DCB Refer Back Same Step Format 2

• System copies DCB parameters from DD statement referenced.

```
//          DCB=*.ddname
```

DCB Refer Back Same Step Example 2

```
//DDOT1    DD  DSN=dataset.name,
//              DISP=(NEW,CATLG,DELETE),
//              UNIT=CART,
//              DCB=(RECFM=FB,LRECL=400,BLKSIZE=0)
...
//DDOT2    DD  DSN=dataset.name,
//              DISP=(NEW,CATLG,DELETE),
//              UNIT=CART,
//              DCB=*.DDOT1
```

DCB Refer-Back Previous Step Format 3

- System copies DCB parameters from DD statement referenced.

```
//pstep1     EXEC PGM=pgmname
//ddnam1     DD   DSN=dataset.name,
...
//                DCB=(RECFM=xx,LRECL=nn,BLKSIZE=nn)
//pstep2     EXEC PGM=pgmname
//ddnam3     DD   DSN=dataset,name,
...
//                DCB=*.pstep1.ddnam1
```

DCB Refer-Back Previous Step Example 3

```
//PS010      EXEC PGM=ABCPGM
//DDOT1      DD   DSN=ABC.SIMPLE1,
...
//                DCB=(RECFM=FB,LRECL=400,BLKSIZE=0
//PS020      EXEC PGM=ABCPGM2
//ddnam3     DD   DSN=ABC.SIMPLE2,
//                DISP=(NEW,CATLG,DELETE),
...
//                DCB=*.PS010.DDOT1
```

DSN Refer-Back Same Step Format 4

- System uses data set name from DD statement referenced.

```
//                DSN=*.ddname
```

DSN Refer-Back Previous Step Format 5

- System uses data set name from DD statement referenced.

```
//                DSN=*.stepa.ddname
```

DSN Refer-Back Same Step Example 4

```
//COB2UCL      PROC
//COB2       EXEC PGM=IGYCRCTL . . .
//SYSLIN     DD   DSN=&&LOADSET . . .
//LKED       EXEC PGM=IEWL . . .
//SYSLIN     DD   DSN=*.COB2.SYSLIN,
...
```

Refer-Backs Multiple PROCs Format 6

• DDs are in different PROCs within the same job:

```
//jobname   JOB …
//step1     EXEC PROC=procnam1
//step2     EXEC PROC=procnam2
//

//procnam1     PROC
//pstepA     EXEC PGM=pgmname
//ddnam1     DD   DSN=dataset.name …

//procnam2     PROC
//pstepB     EXEC PGM=pgmname
//ddnam2     DD   DSN=*.step1.pstepA.ddnam1
//ddnam3     DD   DCB=*.step1.pstepA.ddnam1
```

JES Overview 　　　　　　*5*

- JES the Job Entry Subsystem reads JCL and writes JCL to a DASD spool called the Input queue.

- JES CONVERTER changes JCL to internal text; checks for syntax errors such as a missing comma or misspelled keyword.

- System INITIATOR requests a job to execute.

- JES selects job to execute based upon CLASS and PRIORITY. JES also passes input to the processing program.

- System allocates data sets needed by the job.

- System executes the job.

- JES OUTPUT PROCESSOR writes output to spool called the Output queue.

- JES OUTPUT PROCESSOR prints job output (HARD COPY).

- JES TASK TERMINATOR does job clean-up, also known as purging. JES also writes records to SMF System Management Facilities—SYS1.MAN1, SYS1.MAN2.

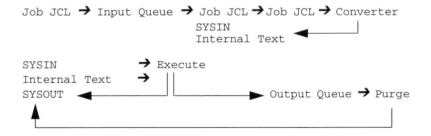

Figure 2 JES and Job Processing

5.1. JES2 VERSUS JES3

• There are 2 types of JES systems available. Most shops use JES2 as opposed to JES3.

1) JES2 can be used for single or multi CPU environments with a maximum of seven operating systems.

• System allocates devices.

• System shop setup controls job mix through classes, and initiators.

• There is independent control over job processing, so jobs can run and print on whatever CPU is available.

2) JES3 is used for a multi CPU environment to present a single system image with a maximum of eight operating systems.

• Can allocate devices needed by job before job runs.

• Controls job mix via job class groups that are defined during JES3 initialization.

• Contains a global JES3 processor with centralized control over job processing. This processor reads all jobs and selects where they will run, and where their output will print.

5.2. JES STATEMENTS

• JES statements can be used to handle input and output processing for the job. JES statements should be coded right after JOB statement, except for Command and PRIORITY. These are coded before the JOB statement. Columns 72-80 and JES statements are ignored in a PROC.

   ☞   Suggest the user not code JES2 command on priority statements. Typically they are not allowed in most shops.

JES2 Statement Format

```
JES2 format is:   /*keyword
```

JES3 Statement Format

```
JES3 format is:  //*keyword
```

JES2 Command Format When N Is in 72 Example

```
/*$command operand[,operand    [comment]    [N]
```

If N is in column 72, the command is not displayed on the master console.

JES2 Command Keywords

```
/*$A|B|C|D|E|F|G|H|I|L|M|N|O|P|R|S|T|TRACE|V|Z
```

JES2 Command Example

Starts initiator 10.

```
/*$SI10
```

Other JES2 Statement Format

```
/*keyword   parameter[,parameter]
```

Other JES2 Statement Keywords

```
/*JOBPARM|MESSAGE|NETACCT|NOTIFY|OUTPUT|
  PRIORITY|ROUTE|SETUP|SIGNOFF|
  SIGNON|XEQ|XMIT
```

JES2 JOBPARM Parameters

```
[BURST|B=Y|N] [,BYTES|M=nnnnnn]
[,CARDS|C=nnnnnnn] [,COPIES|N=nnn]
[,FORMS|F=xxxxxxxx|STD] [,LINECNT|K=nnn]
[,LINES|L=nnnn] [,NOLOG|J]
[,PAGES|G=nnnnn] [,PROCLIB|P=ddname]
[,RESTART|E=Y/N] [,ROOM|R=xxxx]
[,SYSAFF|S=*|ANY|xxxx[,xxxx]
[,TIME|T=nnnn]
```

JES2 JOBPARM Parameters Codes

At least one of the JOBPARM parameters must be coded. Here are the codes:

- B=Y—Cuts output of 3800 into separate sheets.
- B=N—Folds sheets only.
- M—Gives maximum output in thousands of bytes (0-999999).
- C—Gives maximum output cards to punch (0-9999999).
- N—Indicates number of copies of job output to print (1-255).
- F=x...x—Allows up to 8-character special form to print output on.
- STD—Uses default.
- K—Gives maximum lines on an output page, if 0 does not eject to a new page (0-255).
- L—Gives maximum output in thousands of lines (1-9999).
- J—Does not print hard-copy log for job.
- G—Gives maximum number of pages to print for job (1-99999).
- P—Indicates what PROCLIB(s) to search to find the PROC; refers to a DD name in the JES2 PROC.

  ☞ *See: JCLLIB statement.*

- E=Y—Indicates job is executing and a JES warm start occurred. Put job in queue to re-execute.
- N—Do not require job.
- R—Prints up to 4 characters on banner page.
- S—Lists systems that can process the job.
- S=*—System that read job.
- S=ANY—Uses a system in JES2 configuration.
- S=Xxxx—Uses specific system or systems. Code 4-character id of system(s) (can indicate up to 7 systems).
- T—Gives real time of job execution (0-9999). If it exceeded JES2, then it sends a message to operator.

Examples: JES2 JOBPARM

```
/*JOBPARM   PROCLIB=PROC01,ROOM=1234
/*JOBPARM   P=PROC01,R=1234
/*JOBPARM   SYSTEM=ANY
/*JOBPARM   S=SYSA
```

• PROCLIB=PROC01 tells the system to search all PROCLIB libraries concatenated on the PROC01 DD statement in the JES2 PROC for the library that contains the PROC being executed.

> ✍ *See: JES2 PROC Appendix B.*

• ROOM prints on the job banner page and is sometimes used for report distribution.

• SYSTEM=ANY allows the job to run on whatever system is available.

• S=SYSA directs the job to a particular system. Perhaps that is where the data sets for that job reside or that system has superior performance.

Other JES2 Statements

/*MESSAGE—Sends this message to operator console.

/*NETACCT account-number—Supplies account information. Local account information overrides this.

/*NOTIFY node.logonid|node:logonid| node|logonid|node(logonid)|logonid—Indicates to TSO or VM user that the job has ended.

/*OUTPUT code parameter[,parameter…] Specifies characteristics for 1 or more SYSOUTs.

> ✍ *See: OUTPUT JCL Statement.*

/*PRIORITY #—Gives the job a better or lesser position in the input queue. The # is a number from 1-15, normally 15 is the highest priority.

/*ROUTE XEQ name|Nnnnn|node.guestid|
  node:guestid|node|guestid|node(guestid)

/*ROUTE PRINT|PUNCH name|Nnnnn|
  ANYLOCAL|LOCAL|NnRmmmm|
  NnnnRmmm|NnnnnRmm|Rnnnn|
  RMnnnn|RMTnnnn|Unnnn|logonid|
  node.logonid|node:logonid|node|
  logonid|node(logonid)

XEQ—Sends to a specified node to execute.

PRINT|PUNCH—Sends to a specified destination to print
  or punch.

Name—Sends to a specific local device (e.g., name is 1 to 8
  alphanumeric or national characters).

Nnnnn—Sends to a node (e.g., n is 1-1000).

node...guestid—Sends to JES2/3, POWER, or VM system to run.

ANYLOCAL|LOCAL—Sends to local device where job is
  submitted.

NnRmmmm|NnnnRmmm|NnnnRmm—Sends to node and remote
  work station (e.g., n is 1-1000, m is 0-9999 [R0 means local at
  node N...]).

node...logonid—Sends to node and TSO or VM logon.

R...nnnn—Sends to a remote terminal.

Unnnn—Sends to a local terminal.

logonid—Sends to a user's logon id at local node (e.g., JES2
  ROUTE = /*ROUTE PRINT ANYLOCAL).

/*SETUP nnnnnn[,nnnnnn]—Identifies volume serials to mount
  before job executes. Job is automatically put on hold.
  Operator has to release the job to run.

/*SIGNOFF—Ends remote job processing session begun by
  /*SIGNON.

/*SIGNON Rnnnn|RMnnnn|RMTnnnn|
  REMOTEnnn|NxxRnnn|dest|password|
  password2|password3

R...nnnn—See above (must begin in column 16).

dest—Specifies JES2 destination from 1-8 characters (must begin in column 16).

password—Assigns password to connection (must begin in column 25).

password2—Assigns new password for RJE signing on (must begin in column 35).

password3—Gives present password for RJE signing on (must begin in column 73).

/*XEQ Nnnnn|node.guestid—Provides another way of coding /*ROUTE XEQ.

   See: /*ROUTE XEQ above.

/*XMIT Nnnnn|node|node.guestid| node:guestid|node|guestid|node(guestid)| logonid|node.logonid|node:logonid| node|logonid|node(logonid) Transmits records from a JES2 node to another node (e.g., JES2/3, VM).

   See: ROUTE for explanation of parameters.

Notes

• Jes2 statements get a JCL error in an APPC environment.

JCL Examples 6

6.1. ESA V4.1

This chapter gives JCL examples of new parameters and statements introduced with ESA 4.1 and higher versions of the OS/390 system. It includes a comparison between symbolic and the new SET statement, along with sample PROCs comparing older coding techniques to new, how to stack files on a tape, how to efficiently read multiple tape data sets (concatenated input).

ADDRESS Format and Example

- Limit: 60 characters, 4 lines. Line is written on job banner page.

```
//name      OUTPUT ADDRESS=('adres1, . . . adres4')

//A1        OUTPUT ADDRESS=('1880 FULLERTON',
//          'CHICAGO IL')
//REPT10    DD  SYSOUT=A,OUTPUT=(*.A1)
```

BUILDING Format and Example

- Limit: 60 characters, 1 line. Line is written on job banner page.

```
//name      OUTPUT BUILDING='building name'

//B1        OUTPUT BUILDING='A'
//REPT10    DD  SYSOUT=A,OUTPUT=(*.B1)
```

COMMAND Format and Example

- The COMMAND is coded after the JOB statement. Continue by coding to 71. Next line code: // then continue in column 16.

```
//[name]    COMMAND'command,command'

//          COMMAND'VARY 290,OFFLINE'
```

DEPT Format and Example

- Limit: 60 characters, 1 line. Line is written on job banner page.

```
//name       OUTPUT='department'
//D1         OUTPUT  DEPT='M I S'
//REPT1O     DD  SYSOUT=A,OUTPUT=(*.D1)
```

Example: Bldg, Address, Dept

```
//A1         OUTPUT  BUILDING='A',
//           DEPT='M I S',
//           ADDRESS=('1880 FULLERTON',
//           'CHICAGO IL')
//REPT1O     DD  SYSOUT=A,OUTPUT=(*.A1)
```

IF/THEN/ENDIF Format

- Checks highest return code from previous steps. If expression is true, system executes the step.

```
//           IF  (RC oper #) THEN
//step#      EXEC PGM=program
//ddname1    DD  DSN=dataset.name,
...
//           ENDIF
```

IF/THEN/ENDIF Example

- Checks for 0 – 4 as highest return code from previous steps. If expression is true, system executes S10 step.

```
//           IF  (RC LE 4) THEN
//S10        EXEC PGM=ABCPGM
//DDIN       DD  DSN=ABC.SIMPLE,
...
//           ENDIF
```

IF/THEN/ELSE/ENDIF Format

- Checks highest return code from previous steps. If expression is true, system executes the step. If not true, system executes step found after ELSE.

```
//           IF  (RC oper #) THEN
//step#      EXEC PGM=program
//ddname     DD  DSN=dataset.name,
...
//           ELSE
//step#      EXEC PGM=program
//ddname     DD  DSN=dataset.name,
...
//           ENDIF
```

IF/THEN/ELSE/ENDIF Example

- Checks for 0 – 4 as highest return code from previous steps. If expression is true system executes S10 step. If not true, system executes S30 step.

```
//         IF  (RC LT 5)  THEN
//S10       EXEC PGM=program
//DDIN      DD  DSN=ABC.SIMPLE,
...
//         ELSE
//S30       EXEC PGM=program
//DDIN2     DD  DSN=ABC.SIMPLE,
...
//         ENDIF
```

&ᒡ **See:** IF/THEN/ELSE/ENDIF Statement.

INCLUDE Format and Example

- CANNOT code: DD *, DD DATA, JCLLIB, JES2, JES3, JOB, PROC or PEND in INCLUDE member. Copies in JCL.

```
//[name]    INCLUDE MEMBER=mem        [comments]
//UPDAT05   EXEC PGM=pgmname
//         INCLUDE MEMBER=MEM1
//*PUTS JCL FROM MEM1 AFTER EXEC PGM
```

&ᒡ **See:** JCLLIB, below.

JCLLIB Format

- System searches libraries in order found on JCLLIB statement for PROC or INCLUDE members. If not found in either library, system then performs the default PROCLIB search.

- When listing more than 1 library break at the comma, continue next line in columns 4-16.

&ᒡ **See:** JCLLIB Statement.

```
//[name]    JCLLIB  ORDER=(library1,library2,...)
```

JCLLIB Example

- System searches—PROD.PROCLIB, PROD.INCLIB, then system default.

```
//PAW010    JOB ...
//         JCLLIB ORDER=(PROD.PROCLIB,
//         PROD.INCLIB)
```

NAME Format and Example

- Limit: 60 characters, 1 line. Line is written on job banner page.

```
//name     OUTPUT NAME='person''s name'
//N1       OUTPUT NAME='BRITTANI WEBER'
//REPT1O   DD  SYSOUT=A,OUTPUT=(*.N1)
```

NOTIFY Format and Example

- Can specify up to four logon ids.

```
//name     OUTPUT NOTIFY=([node.]logon...)
//Y1       OUTPUT NOTIFY=(TPGM001)
```

OUTDISP Format and Example

- OUTDISP happens at job end. If OUTDISP is not coded, system uses shop's default — normally deletes job SYSOUT from the JES queue once the job prints. If abnormal is not coded, it defaults to normal.

  - KEEP—Directs SYSOUT to Output queue with ODISP of KEEP; after it prints, moves to Held queue with ODISP of LEAVE.

  - LEAVE—Directs output to Held queue. When released to Output queue, changes ODISP to KEEP; after printed, moves to Held with ODISP of LEAVE.

  - WRITE—Prints and deletes SYSOUT output.

  - HOLD—Stays in JES HOLD queue until released to output queue to print or until purged.

  - PURGE—Deletes SYSOUT output without printing.

```
//name     OUTPUT   OUTDISP=(normal,abend)
//DSP1     OUTPUT   OUTDISP=(WRITE,KEEP)
//REPT1O   DD   SYSOUT=A,OUTPUT=(*.DSP1)
//DSP2     OUTPUT   OUTDISP=WRITE
//REPT11   DD   SYSOUT=A,OUTPUT=(*.DSP2)
```

ROOM Format and Example

- Limit: 60 characters, 1 line. Line is written on job banner page.

```
//name      OUTPUT='room'

//RM1       OUTPUT  ROOM='A10'
//REPT1O    DD  SYSOUT=A,OUTPUT=(*.RM1)
```

SEGMENT Format

- Releases pages to print every # number of pages. SEGMENT overrides SPIN.

```
//ddname    DD  SYSOUT=class,SEGMENT=#pages
```

SEGMENT Example

- Every time 200 pages are created, they are released to print (can print on different printers if printers are set to same class).

```
//REPT1O    DD  SYSOUT=A,SEGMENT=200
```

SET Format

```
//[name]    SET symbolic='value',symbolic2='value2'
```

- System uses the last SET statement to give a value to the symbolic. SET statements give the user a way to code a symbolic with plain JCL.

☞ Suggest user not code SET statements with cataloged procedures.

🔗 **See:** SET Statement.

SET Example

```
//          SET LIB='PROD'
//UPDAT05   EXEC PGM=pgm1
//STEPLIB   DD  DSN=&LIB..LOAD,...  *ASSIGNED PROD
//REPRT10   EXEC PGM=pgm2
//          SET LIB='TEST'
//STEPLIB   DD  DSN=&LIB..LOAD,...  *ASSIGNED TEST
```

- System looks for PGM1 in library PROD.LOAD
- System looks for PGM2 in library TEST.LOAD

Symbolic Format

```
//          symbolic='value'
```

Symbolic Compared with SET

*   Symbolic values coded on the EXEC PROC statement in the JCL that calls the PROC to run override values coded in the cataloged procedure on the PROC label statement.

*   With SET the last SET statement value is used so the user cannot override the SET statement.

Symbolic Example

*   JCL that calls PROC to run

```
//JS001      EXEC PROC=PAW010,
//               LIB='QUAL'    *OVERRIDES PROC
//

//PAW010    PROC LIB='PROD'    *PROC LABEL
//UPDAT05   EXEC PGM=pgmname
//STEPLIB   DD   DSN=&LIB..LOAD,... *ASSIGNED QUAL
```

*   System uses override symbolic, QUAL.LOAD

SPIN Format and Example 1

*   SPIN=NO—means print at end of job. This is the default. UNNALLOC—Starts printing at end of step. SEGMENT overrides SPIN.

```
//ddname    DD  SYSOUT=class,SPIN=value
//REPT10    DD  SYSOUT=A,SPIN=UNALLOC
```

SPIN Example 2

*   Print when data set is closed instead of end of step.

```
//REPT10    DD  SYSOUT=A,SPIN=UNALLOC,
//              FREE=CLOSE
```

TIME Format and Examples

```
//          TIME=value
//          TIME=NOLIMIT    or
//          TIME=MAXIMUM
```

TITLE Format and Example

* Limit: 60 characters, 1 line. Line is written on job banner page.

```
//name       OUTPUT    TITLE='title'

//T1         OUTPUT    TITLE='DIRECTOR'
//REPT1O     DD   SYSOUT=A,OUTPUT=(*.T1)
```

USERLIB Format and Example

* PSF searches libraries on USERLIB only if PAGEDEF = member parameter is also coded. Otherwise, the system searches system libraries.

```
//name       OUTPUT PAGEDEF=member,
//           USERLIB=(library1,library2)

//ULIB       OUTPUT FORMDEF=name,
//           PAGEDEF=STD1,
//           USERLIB=(PROD.USERLIB)
```

6.2. ESA V4.2

Action to Take If Output Is Exceeded

- Code on JOB statement. If not coded, uses system default. This controls output for the job. #—Means 0-999999, maximum BYTES in thousands to print (800 means 800,000).

BYTES Format and Example

```
//                 BYTES=# | [ (#,CANCEL|DUMP|WARNING)]
//jobname JOB  (accounting),'programmer name',
//                 BYTES=(800,WARNING)
```

CARDS Format and Example

- #—Means 0-999999—JES2, # = 0-6500000—JES3, maximum number of CARDS to punch (800).

```
//                 CARDS=# | [ (#,CANCEL|DUMP|WARNING)]
//                 CARDS=(1000,WARNING)
```

LINES Format and Example

- #—Means 0-999999, maximum LINES in thousands to print (100 means 100,000).

```
//                 LINES=# | [ (#,CANCEL|DUMP|WARNING)]
//                 LINES=(100,WARNING)
```

PAGES Format and Example

- #—Means 0-999999, maximum PAGES to print (5,000).

```
//                 PAGES=# | [ (#,CANCEL|DUMP|WARNING)]
//                 PAGES=(5000,WARNING)
```

&SYSUID Format and Example

- User codes in the JCL anywhere user's logon id might be coded, and the system replaces &SYSUID with the submitter's logon id.

```
//ddname    DD  DSN=&SYSUID..dataset.name, ...
```

6.3. SAMPLE PROC—OLDER CODING TECHNIQUES

JCL That calls PROC to Run

```
//PPAY010   JOB (540,77),'PAY UPDATE',
//             CLASS=A,
//             MSGCLASS=C
/*JOBPARM  P=PROC01         *OLDER CODING
//JOBLIB    DD  DSN=PROD.LOADLIB,
//             DISP=SHR
//S001      EXEC PROC=PAY010
//
```

Cataloged Procedure (PROC)

```
//PAY010    PROC DSN='PAYP',
//             OUT='C'
//* * * * * * * * * * * * * * * * * * * * * * * *
//*UPDATE-VSAM,RESTORE JOB-PPAY010R
//* * * * * * * * * * * * * * * * * * * * * * * *
//PS010     EXEC PGM=PAYUPDT
//PAYI      DD  DSN=&DSN..GDG.HRS(0),
//             DISP=(OLD,KEEP,KEEP)
//REPTO     DD  DSN=&DSN..WRK.REPTS,
//             DISP=(NEW,CATLG,DELETE),
//             SPACE=(CYL,(10,2),RLSE),
//             DCB=(RECFM=FB,LRECL=133,BLKSIZE=28329)
//MASTO     DD  DSN=&DSN..GDG.HRS(+1),
//             DISP=(NEW,CATLG,DELETE),
//             UNIT=(TAPE,,DEFER),
//             LABEL=EXPDT=99000,
//             DCB=(P.MODL,RECFM=VB,LRECL=1024,BLKSIZE=31872)
//SYSOUT    DD  SYSOUT=*
//SYSUDUMP  DD  SYSOUT=D
//* * * * * * * * * * * * * * * * * * * * * * * *
//*PRINT REPORTS
//* * * * * * * * * * * * * * * * * * * * * * * *
//PS020     EXEC PGM=PRTPGM,
//             COND=(0,NE)
//REPTI     DD  DSN=&DSN..WRK.REPTS,
//             DISP=(OLD,DELETE,KEEP)
//REPTO     DD  SYSOUT=&OUT
//SYSUDUMP  DD  SYSOUT=D
```

- Compare this with the "Sample PROC Using ESA V4 and SMS" that follows.

- Items underlined indicate older coding techniques.

6.4. SAMPLE PROC USING ESA V4 AND SMS

JCL That calls PROC to Run

```
//PPAY010   JOB (540,77),'PAY UPDATE',
//          CLASS=A,
//          MSGCLASS=C
//          JCLLIB ORDER=(P.PROCLIB,P.INCLIB) *ESA
//JOBLIB    DD  DSN=PROD.LOADLIB,
//          DISP=SHR
//S001      EXEC PROC=PAY010
//
```

Cataloged Procedure (PROC)

```
//PAY010    PROC DSN='PAYP',
//          OUT='C'
//* * * * * * * * * * * * * * * * * * * * * * * *
//*UPDATE-VSAM,RESTORE JOB-PPAY010R
//* * * * * * * * * * * * * * * * * * * * * * * *
//PS010     EXEC PGM=PAYUPDT
//PAYI      DD  DSN=&DSN..GDG.HRS(0),
//          DISP=(OLD,KEEP,KEEP)
//REPTO     DD  DSN=&DSN..WRK.REPTS,
//          DISP=(NEW,CATLG,DELETE),
//          AVGREC=K,              *SMS
//          SPACE=(133,(100,10),RLSE),
//          RECFM=FB,LRECL=133     *ESA
//MASTO     DD  DSN=&DSN..GDG.HRS(+1),
//          DISP=(NEW,CATLG,DELETE),
//          UNIT=(CART,,DEFER),
//          EXPDT=99000,           *ESA
//          RECFM=VB,LRECL=1024    *ESA&SMS
...
//* * * * * * * * * * * * * * * * * * * * * * * *
//*PRINT REPORTS
//* * * * * * * * * * * * * * * * * * * * * * * *
//          IF  (RC EQ 0)  THEN    *ESA
//PS020     EXEC PGM=PRTPGM
//REPTI     DD  DSN=&DSN..WRK.REPTS,
//          DISP=(OLD,DELETE,KEEP)
//REPTO     DD  SYSOUT=&OUT
//SYSUDUMP  DD  SYSOUT=D
//          ENDIF                  *ESA
```

Notes

- ESA V4—JCLLIB is coded instead of JOBPARM. IF... instead of COND. Can still code COND but IF is easier to understand.

- SMS—AVGREC is used and model DSCB is not needed when creating a +1 generation data set.

- ESA—DCB, LABEL, and block size are not needed. System blocks half track for DASD, 32K for tape. Larger block sizes reduce I/O so job will run faster.

- CA-1—For production, if shop is using the Retention Data Set (RDS), then EXPDT = 99000 is not coded in the JCL. Instead, the programmer fills out a form specifying retention then the RDS is updated by someone in operations or technical support.

6.5. TAPE FILE STACKING: ESA V4 & SMS (REF & RETAIN)

```
//COPY10    EXEC PGM=SORT
//* * * * * * * * * * * * * * * * * * * * * * * * *
//* CREATE A COPY FOR ANOTHER DEPARTMENT
//* * * * * * * * * * * * * * * * * * * * * * * * *
//SORTIN    DD  DSN=PAPG.HR(0),DISP=OLD
//SYSIN     DD  *
    SORT FIELDS=COPY
/*
//SORTOUT   DD  DSN=PAPG.HR.COPY(+1),
//              DISP=(NEW,CATLG,DELETE),
//              UNIT=CART,
//              VOL=(,RETAIN,,99),
//              LABEL=(1,SL,EXPDT=99000),
//              RECFM=VB,LRECL=10300,BLKSIZE=0 *ESA&SMS
//SYSOUT    DD  SYSOUT=*
//* * * * * * * * * * * * * * * * * * * * * * * * *
//* CREATE A COPY FOR ANOTHER DEPARTMENT
//* * * * * * * * * * * * * * * * * * * * * * * * *
//          IF  (RC LE 0)  THEN
//COPY20    EXEC PGM=SORT
//SORTIN    DD  DSN=PAPG.AD(0),DISP=OLD
//SYSIN     DD  *
    SORT FIELDS=COPY
/*
//SORTOUT   DD  DSN=PAPG.AD.COPY(+1),
//              DISP=(NEW,CATLG,DELETE),
//              UNIT=CART,
//              VOL=(,RETAIN,,99,REF=*.COPY10.SORTOUT),
//              LABEL=(2,SL,EXPDT=99000),
//              RECFM=FB,LRECL=80,BLKSIZE=0
//SYSOUT    DD  SYSOUT=*
//          ENDIF
//* * * * * * * * * * * * * * * * * * * * * * * * *
//* CREATE A COPY FOR ANOTHER DEPARTMENT
//* * * * * * * * * * * * * * * * * * * * * * * * *
//          IF  (RC LE 0)  THEN
//COPY30    EXEC PGM=SORT
//SORTIN    DD  DSN=PAPG.OT(0),DISP=OLD
//SYSIN     DD  *
    SORT FIELDS=COPY
/*
//SORTOUT   DD  DSN=PAPG.OT.BK(+1),
//              DISP=(NEW,CATLG,DELETE),
//              UNIT=CART,
//              VOL=(,,,99,REF=*.COPY20.SORTOUT),
//              LABEL=(3,SL,EXPDT=99000),
//              RECFM=FB,LRECL=80
//SYSOUT    DD  SYSOUT=*
//          ENDIF
```

Notes

> &⁄ **See:** Notes from previous Example 6.4.

- This example is "PLAIN JCL" not a cataloged procedure.
- Data sets being backed up should have the same retention period.
- If a copy of the physical sequential data set is needed, and not a backup, then use SORT instead of IEBGENER— performance is better. Some shops will automatically invoke SORT for IEBGENER.
- If user is creating a backup of data sets and not a copy for use by another group: shop should have an efficient package to perform backups, such as IBM's DF/DSS program ADRDSSU or Innovation Data Processing's program FDR.
  These packages back up all types of data sets such as VSAM, generation data sets, simple or physical sequential flat files, and partitioned data sets.

> &⁄ **See:** DF/DSS.

6.6. TAPE CONCATENATION: (UNIT=AFF)

```
//PRNT010  EXEC PGM=IEBGENER
//** ** ** ** ** ** ** ** ** **
//*  READ & PRINT 3 TAPE DATA SETS
//** ** ** ** ** ** ** ** ** **
//SYSIN    DD  DUMMY
//SYSUT1   DD  DSN=PAYPRD.GDG.HRS(0),
//             DISP=(OLD,KEEP,KEEP)
//         DD  DSN=PAYPRD.GDG.EMP(0),
//             DISP=(OLD,KEEP,KEEP),
//             UNIT=AFF=SYSUT1
//         DD  DSN=PAYPRD.GDG.OT(0),
//             DISP=(OLD,KEEP,KEEP),
//             UNIT=AFF=SYSUT1
//SYSUT2   DD  SYSOUT=C
//SYSPRINT DD  SYSOUT=*
```

- UNIT=AFF=SYSUT1—Asks the system to use same tape drive to mount tapes as opposed to asking for multiple drives and holding valuable system resources. Since the first tape must be read before the second tape can be read this is an efficient coding technique.

Often Used Utilities 7

This chapter gives JCL examples of commonly used utilities with a very brief explanation of control statements and suggestions for more efficient use. In-depth coverage is beyond the scope of this book. Utilities covered are:

- IBM's ADRDSSU to back up and restore application data sets.

- ICETOOL to copy entire data sets or select certain records within a data set.

- IDCAMS to build or delete a GDG base, or print a physical sequential data set.

- Using IDCAMS for VSAM data sets—delete and define, copy, change the data set name or print a data set.

- IEBGENER to write physical sequential data sets and members of a PDS to DASD or directly to the printer.

- IEFBR14 to delete simple cataloged data sets.

- SORT to sequence records.

7.1. IBM'S DF/DSS EFFICIENT BACKUP

- Use IBM's DF/DSS program ADRDSSU to efficiently back up application data sets. Back up all types of data sets such as VSAM, physical sequential (simple and GDG), libraries—PDS and PDSE.

- Performs file stacking of data sets to tape. Return code of 0 is a good return code. Return code of 8 can mean a data set was not backed up.

7.1.1. DF/DSS—ADRDSSU Back-up Example

```
//PBRIT4    JOB (PR,34IS,,999),'BACKUP ADRDSSU',
//          CLASS=4,
//          MSGCLASS=X,
//          REGION=4M,
//          NOTIFY=&SYSUID
//*****************************************
//*CREATES 2 BACKUP DATA SETS WITH 1 RUN--RC=0
//*RC-8 MEANS FILE(S) WERE NOT BACKED UP
//*USE ADRDSSU TO RESTORE DATA SET BEFORE USING
//*  BACKS UP THE FOLLOWING DATA SETS
//*          -- PROD.JCLCLASS.DATA
//*          -- PROD.JCLCLASS.GDG(0)
//*****************************************
//BACK05    EXEC PGM=ADRDSSU
//SYSIN     DD  *
          DUMP OUTDD(BACKOUT, BACKOUT2)      -
               DS(INCLUDE(                   -
               PROD.JCLCLASS.DATA            -
               PROD.JCLCLASS.GDG(0)          -
               ))                            -
          OPT(4)
     *READ CYL REDUCE I-O—THIS IS A COMMENT*/
/*
//BACKOUT   DD  DSN=PROD.CLASS.DSSBKUP(+1),
//              DISP=(NEW,CATLG,DELETE),
//              UNIT=CART,
//              VOL=(,,,99),    *> 5 CARTS
//              EXPDT=99000     *RETENTION
//BACKOUT2 DD  DSN=PROD.CLASS.DSSVAULT(+1),
//              DISP=(NEW,CATLG,DELETE),
//              UNIT=CART,
//              VOL=(,,,99),    *> 5 CARTS
//              EXPDT=99000     *RETENTION
//SYSPRINT DD  SYSOUT=*
//
```

- "Plain JCL" to back up 2 data sets. Must receive a return code of 0 for successful completion.

- Other jobs cannot be accessing a data set being backed up.

- Creates 2 output data sets indicated by BACKOUT and BACKOUT2.

- VOL=(,,,99)—Allows system to write to more than 5 tape volumes without abending.

- EXPDT=99000—Sets CA-1 retention. This is site-specific. See shop JCL standards.

☞ Suggest user key the exact data set name to be backed up. Must use ADRDSSU to restore before using the backed-up data sets. Always check for a return code of 0 to ensure all data sets were backed up.

- SYSIN—Reads control statements for program ADRDSSU.

- DUMP—Means back up.

- OUTDD—Specifies JCL DD statement ddname(s) for output.

- DS INCLUDE—Specifies Data Sets (DS) to back up.

- Dash—Indicates a control statement continuation. List data sets as shown.

- OPT(4)—Reads entire cylinder to reduce I/O.

- /* */—Indicates a control statement comment.

- ALLDATA—Physical data set restore preserves original size of the data set.

- SPHERE—Captures and will restore all AIX clusters and paths (use with VSAM data sets).

- SYSPRINT—Specifies statement where utility messages are printed.

For additional information on any IBM products access IBM's Book Manager READ. This product gives on-line access to IBM manuals. There is a mainframe version of the product that the user would find as an option off one of their TSO/ISPF panels. There is also a PC version called the OS/390 Collection containing every OS/390 IBM manual a user could need on 6 CD-ROMs.

7.1.2. DF/DSS—ADRDSSU Example to Restore

- Use IBM's DF/DSS program ADRDSSU to restore application data sets backed up using ADRDSSU. Back up all types of data sets such as VSAM, physical sequential (simple and GDG), libraries—PDS and PDSE.

```
//PROD4     JOB (PR,34IS,,999),'RESTORE ADRDSSU',
//          CLASS=4,
//          MSGCLASS=X,
//          REGION=4M,
//          NOTIFY=&SYSUID
//**********************************************
//*DF/DSS-ADRDSSU-RESTORE APPLICATION DATA SETS
//*    RESTORE ONE FILE OR ALL FILES -- GOOD RC=0
//**********************************************
//REST05    EXEC PGM=ADRDSSU
//SYSIN     DD  *
          RESTORE  INDD(RESTIN)           -
                   DS(INCLUDE(            -
                   PROD.JCLCLASS.DATA     -
                   PROD.JCLCLASS.GDG(0)   -
                   ))                     -
                   REPLACE  /*IF DSN EXISTS*/    -
                   CATALOG  /*IF DSN DOES NOT EXIST*/
/*
//RESTIN    DD  DSN= PROD.CLASS.DSSBKUP(+0), INPUT
//              DISP=SHR
//SYSPRINT  DD  SYSOUT=*
//
```

- SYSIN—Reads control statements for program ADRDSSU.

- RESTORE—Means copy data sets to DASD.

- INDD—Specifies JCL DD statement ddname for input.

- DS INCLUDE—Specifies Data Sets (DS) to back up.

- Dash—Indicates a control statement continuation.

- REPLACE—Indicates if data set exists write over it.

- CATALOG—Indicates if data set does not exist, catalog so system can easily find the data set.

- /* */—Indicates a control statement comment.

- SYSPRINT—Specifies statement where utility messages are printed.

7.2. DFSORT ICETOOL

- IBM'S DFSORT ICETOOL copies data sets and has various options to select certain fields or records, to count: records, unique values in a field, or values within a certain range. Also invokes DFSORT to sort.

```
//ICE10     EXEC PGM=ICETOOL
//TOOLIN    DD  *     *CONTROL STATEMENTS
            COPY FROM(ddin)    -
            TO(ddout)
/*
//ddin      DD  DSN=data.set.in,          *INPUT DD
//              DISP=SHR
//ddout     DD  DSN=copied.data.set.out,  *OUTPUT DD
//              DISP=(NEW,CATLG,DELETE),
//              SPACE=(132,(100,10),RLSE),
//              AVGREC=K,                  *SMS
//              RECFM=FB,LRECL=132,BLKSIZE=0  *ESA
//DFMSG      DD  SYSOUT=*    *DFSORT MESSAGES
//TOOLMSG    DD  SYSOUT=*    *ICETOOL MESSAGES
```

- Copies input data set to output data set.

- TOOLIN—Reads ICETOOL control statements. Copies input to output. To continue the control statement, code a space and a dash.

- Ddin—Names input data set and must be the same as specified in the control statement COPY FROM.

- Ddout—Names output data set and must be the same as specified in the control statement COPY ... TO.

- DFMSG—Prints SORT messages.

- TOOLMSG—Prints ICETOOL messages.

7.2.1. ICETOOL SELECT Control Statement

`SELECT FROM(ddin) TO(ddout) ON(start,length,format) option`

• Selects and copies records from input to output.

  • Start—Indicates beginning byte.

  • Length—Indicates number of bytes.

  • Format—Indicates field format. Most often used formats are: CH for character, PD for signed packed decimal, ZD for signed zoned decimal.

• Option—Indicates the basis for selecting the records.

  • ALLDUPS—Selects records where the same value occurs more than once in the field.

  • NODUPS—Selects records where field value occurs once.

  • HIGHER(n)—Selects records where the same field value occurs more than *n* (1-99) times.

  • LOWER(n)—Selects records where the same field value occurs less than *n* (1-99) times.

  • EQUAL(n)—Selects records where the same field value occurs *n* (1-99) times.

  • FIRST—Selects first record where the same field value occurs more than once.

  • LAST—Selects last record where the same field value occurs more than once.

7.3. IDCAMS BUILD GDG BASE—PLAIN JCL

- Run IDCAMS once to identify a data set as a generation data
  group (GDG) to the system.

```
//PBHCW1    JOB (4887,12),'BUILD BASE',
//              CLASS=A,
//              NOTIFY=PBHCW,
//              MSGCLASS=X
//*************************************************
//* BUILD GDG BASE
//*************************************************
//BLDGDG1   EXEC PGM=IDCAMS
//SYSIN     DD  *
     DEFINE GDG                            -
        (NAME(PAYP.GDG.MASTER)             -
        NOEMPTY                            -
        SCRATCH     /*TAPE TOO*/           -
        LIMIT(7))
/*
//SYSPRINT DD  SYSOUT=*
//
```

- DD statements required by IDCAMS are:

  - SYSIN—Reads control statements.

  - SYSPRINT—Prints utility output and messages.

- DEFINE GDG—Indicates create the GDG base entry.

- NAME—Identifies the data set name.

- EMPTY—Uncatalogs ALL generations.

- NOEMPTY—Uncatalogs OLDEST generation (use 99.9%).

- SCRATCH—Deletes from VTOC; frees space.

- NOSCRATCH—Does not delete DASD data set from VTOC or
  free the space. This can be used for tape data sets.

- LIMIT—Gives number of generation data sets wanted.

  ☞   Suggest always using SCRATCH. This will not hurt
     anything and user can easily switch media.

- /*TAPE TOO*/— Is a control statement comment. These begin
  with /* and end with */. Must have a space before /* and after */

- DASH is used to indicate a continuation for IDCAMS control
  statements

7.3.1. IDCAMS Delete GDG Base—Plain JCL

*   Delete all generation data sets first. TSO/ISPF screen 3.4 will allow you to do this if you have the authority.

*   Run IDCAMS to remove generation data group base entry.

```
//PBHCW1    JOB (4887,12),'DELETE BASE',
//             CLASS=A,
//             NOTIFY=PBHCW,
//             MSGCLASS=X
//*********************************************
//* BUILD GDG BASE
//*********************************************
//DELBASE   EXEC PGM=IDCAMS
//SYSIN     DD   *
     DELETE (PAYP.GDG.MASTER)    -
     GDG
/*
//SYSPRINT DD  SYSOUT=*
//
```

*   DD statements required by IDCAMS are:

    *   SYSIN—Reads control statements.

    *   SYSPRINT—Prints utility output and messages.

*   DELETE …GDG—Removes the base entry.

7.4. IDCAMS DEFINE KEY-SEQUENCED DATA SET

When creating a VSAM data set the following must be done:

1) DELETE existing VSAM data set.

2) DEFINE the VSAM data set.

3) REPRO copy data to the VSAM data set.

• The first time, the VSAM data set won't be there to delete and AMS passes a return code 8. IF LASTCC . . . changes, return code to 0.

• This is a quick sample for defining a VSAM data set. There are many other control statements available. For more information see IBM's Access Method Services manuals.

CONTROL STATEMENT	MEANING
• DEFINE CLUSTER	Tells AMS to define a VSAM data set.
• NAME(cluster.name)	Defines the VSAM data set name.
• DATASET(ddname)	Refers to columns 3–10 in the JCL DD.
• VOLUMES(vol-ser)	Tells AMS where to create data set; may not need if shop has SMS.
• INDEXED—KSDS	Key Sequenced can be processed sequentially or randomly.
• NOINDEXED—ESDS	Entry Sequenced is processed sequentially.
• NUMBERED—RRDS	Relative Record is processed on relative position in data set.
• LINEAR—LDS	Linear Data set can be processed via Data Windowing Services with High Level Languages or via the Assembler language.

- KEYS(length offset)   Defines the key.
  - Length   Key size in bytes.
  - Offset   Skip # bytes (if key is in columns 5–10, code: KEYS(6 4).
- DATA   Defines characteristics of *DATA* portion of VSAM cluster.
  - NAME   Gives data set DATA name.
  (cluster.name.DATA)
    - RECORDS   Gives data set size in records.
    - TRACKS   Gives data set size in tracks.
    (primary, secondary)
    - CYLINDERS   Gives data set size in cylinders (preferred—more efficient).
- RECORDSIZE (avg max)   Gives average and maximum record lengths.
- CISZ (####)   Indicates Control Interval Size.

☞ Suggest 4096 as the best balance for most data sets.

- INDEX   Defines characteristics of INDEX portion of VSAM cluster.
  - NAME   Gives data set INDEX name.
  (cluster.name.INDEX)
  - /* code comments */   Code comments in control statements.
  - Dash   Is used to indicate a continuation for IDCAMS control statements.

7.4.1. IDCAMS Delete & Define KSDS Example

```
//*************************************************
//* DELETE & DEFINE VSAM FILE
//*************************************************
//STEP01    EXEC PGM=IDCAMS
//SYSIN     DD  *
        /* DELETE PAYROLL MASTER */
        DELETE                           -
            (PAYT.VSM.MASTER)    -
            PURGE                -
            CLUSTER
        IF  LASTCC LT  9                 -
             THEN  SET  MAXCC=0
        /*  DEFINE PAYROLL MASTER  */
        DEFINE  CLUSTER                          -
            (NAME(PAYP.VSM.MASTER)               -
            VOLUMES(V80S02)                      -
            INDEXED                              -
            KEYS(9 4))    /*  ACCOUNT #  */  -
        DATA                                     -
            (NAME(PAYP.VSM.MASTER.DATA)          -
            CYLINDERS(100)                       -
            RECORDSIZE(100 400))             -
        INDEX                                    -
            (NAME(PAYP.VSM.MASTER.INDEX))
    /*
//SYSPRINT DD  SYSOUT=*
```

* DD statements required by IDCAMS are:

  * SYSIN—Reads control statements.

  * SYSPRINT—Prints utility output and messages.

* DELETE ...PURGE CLUSTER—Removes the VSAM data set.

* IF...—Sets a 0 return code instead of an 8 if data set is not found for the DELETE.

* DEFINE...—Creates the new cluster.

7.4.2. IDCAMS REPRO: Copy to a VSAM Data Set

- Plain JCL to run IDCAMS to copy data to a VSAM data set. IDCAMS can also copy to a physical sequential data set or member of a PDS.

```
//PBHCW1    JOB (4887,12),'COPY',
//          CLASS=A,
//          NOTIFY=PBHCW,
//          MSGCLASS=X
//************************************************
//* COPY OR LOAD DATA TO VSAM FILE
//************************************************
//STEP01    EXEC PGM=IDCAMS
//INDD      DD DSN=PAYP.GDG.MASTER.BKUP(+0),
//          DISP=SHR
//OUTDD     DD DSN=PAYP.VSM.MASTER,
//          DISP=SHR
//SYSIN     DD *
   REPRO                 -
           INFILE(INDD)  -
           OUTFILE(OUTDD)
/*
//SYSPRINT DD  SYSOUT=*
//
```

- DD statements required by IDCAMS are:

  - SYSIN—Reads control statements.

  - SYSPRINT—Prints utility output and messages.

- REPRO—Copies the data set.

- INFILE—Defines ddname (columns 3-10) of input data set.

- OUTFILE—Defines ddname (columns 3-10) of output data set.

- PAYP.VSM.MASTER VSAM dataset was created in the previous example.

7.5. IDCAMS ALTER: RENAME A VSAM DATA SET

- Plain JCL to run IDCAMS to change the VSAM data set name.

```
//PBHCW1    JOB (4887,12),'RENAME',
//              CLASS=A,
//              NOTIFY=PBHCW,
//              MSGCLASS=X
//***********************************************
//* RENAME A VSAM FILE
//***********************************************
//STEP01    EXEC PGM=IDCAMS
//SYSIN     DD  *
   ALTER                               -
           PAYP.VSM.MASTER             -
           NEWNAME(PAYT.VSM.MASTER)
/*
//SYSPRINT DD  SYSOUT=*
//
```

- DD statements required by IDCAMS are:

  - SYSIN—Reads control statements.

  - SYSPRINT—Prints utility output and messages.

- ALTER—Changes data set name if user has authority.

- User can also use IDCAMS to change the name of non-VSAM data sets.

7.6. IDCAMS DELETE: NON-VSAM DATA SETS

```
//PBHCW1    JOB (4887,12),'DELETE',
//             CLASS=A,
//             NOTIFY=PBHCW,
//             MSGCLASS=X
//************************************************
//* DELETE PHYSICAL SEQUENTIAL
//************************************************
//STEP01    EXEC PGM=IDCAMS
//SYSIN     DD  *
     /* DELETE PAYROLL MASTER */

     DELETE                        -
          (data.set.name)
/*
//SYSPRINT DD  SYSOUT=*
```

- DD statements required by IDCAMS are:

  - SYSIN—Reads control statements.

  - SYSPRINT—Prints utility output and messages.

- DELETE …—Deletes and uncatalogs a physical sequential data set or a Partitioned Data Set (PDS).

```
     DELETE                   -
          (library(member))
```

- DELETE …—Deletes a member from a Partitioned Data Set (PDS).

7.7. IDCAMS PRINT: PRINT VSAM OR SEQUENTIAL DATA SET

- Plain JCL to run IDCAMS to print a VSAM or physical sequential data set, or member of a PDS.

```
//PBHCW1    JOB (4887,12),'PRINT DATA SET',
//          CLASS=A,
//          NOTIFY=PBHCW,
//          MSGCLASS=X
//***********************************************
//* PRINT DATA SET
//***********************************************
//STEP01    EXEC PGM=IDCAMS
//PRTIN1    DD  DSN=PAYP.VSM.MASTER,
//          DISP=SHR
//SYSIN     DD  *
   PRINT                           -
             INFILE(PRTIN1)        -
             CHARACTER
/*
//SYSPRINT DD  SYSOUT=*
//
```

- DD statements required by IDCAMS are:

  - SYSIN—Reads control statements.

  - SYSPRINT—Prints utility output and messages.

- PRINT...CHARACTER—Prints contents of data set in character format.

- INFILE—Defines ddname (columns 3-10) of input data set.

Notes

- The following control statement can also be used: INDATASET('PAYP.VSM.MASTER')

7.8. IEFBR14 CLEANS UP CATALOGED SIMPLE (PS) DATA SETS

```
//CLEAN05  EXEC PGM=IEFBR14
//DD1      DD   DSN=dataset.name1,
//              DISP=(MOD,DELETE,DELETE),
//              UNIT=SYSDA,
//              SPACE=(TRK,(0))
//DD2      DD   DSN=dataset.name2,
//              DISP=(MOD,DELETE,DELETE),
//              UNIT=SYSDA,
//              SPACE=(TRK,(0))
```

• Deletes and uncatalogs physical sequential flat data sets. User can code at the beginning of the job for test jobs or place before each step with condition checks to allow step restart if your shop does not have an automated restart software package.

• If your shop has SMS, the UNIT and SPACE parameters may not need to be coded (depends on how SMS is implemented). Try it.

• Use to clean up physical sequential (flat files only—do NOT code to delete a member from a library, as system works on a data set level and will delete the entire library if user has the authority).

• Code MOD because if data set does not exist, the system first creates and then deletes the data set. Therefore, the clean-up step will not JCL error with Data Set Not Found.

• There are several restart rerun automated software packages available to perform this task in a production environment (e.g., ZEBB from Platinum Technologies; CA-11 from Computer Associates).

7.9. IEBGENER WRITING TO DASD

- IEBGENER is the most commonly used IBM utility. IEBGENER copies physical sequential data sets—including members of a PDS, can print up to 132 characters, can change the record or block length, can add members to PDS, can also edit or reorganize records in sequential data set.

- When SYSIN DD DUMMY is coded, IEBGENER copies SYSUT1 DD to SYSUT2 DD. Some shops automatically invoke ICEGENER (SORT to perform the copy, as SORT is more efficient than IEBGENER).

```
//PBHCW1    JOB  (4887,12),'COPY',
//           CLASS=A,
//           NOTIFY=PBHCW,
//           MSGCLASS=X
//*************************************************
//* COPY SYSUT1 TO SYSUT2
//*************************************************
//GENER05   EXEC PGM=IEBGENER
//SYSIN     DD   DUMMY                *CONTROL STATEMENTS
//SYSUT1    DD   DSN=data.set.in,     *INPUT DD
//               DISP=SHR
//SYSUT2    DD   DSN=copied.data.set.out,   *OUTPUT DD
//               DISP=(NEW,CATLG,DELETE),
//               SPACE=(132,(100,10),RLSE),
//               AVGREC=K,                    *SMS
//               RECFM=FB,LRECL=132,BLKSIZE=0  *ESA
//SYSPRINT  DD   SYSOUT=*    *UTILITY MESSAGES
```

To write output directly to printer, replace the SYSUT2 DD with:

```
//SYSUT2    DD   SYSOUT=*    *WRITES TO PRINTER
```

7.10. SORT USING ESA AND SMS

* Sort is used to re-sequence data sets. SYSIN DD reads sort control statements. In the example below, sort starting in column 1 for 20 bytes in ascending sequence, CH = character format.

* SORTIN DD reads input data set to be sorted.

* If sort work files are needed, up to 16 can be coded, i.e., SORTWK01 to SORTWK16.

* SORTOUT DD is where sort writes sorted output data set. SPACE, RECFM, LRECL will vary according to data set characteristics.

* SYSOUT DD is where sort writes sort messages.

```
//PBHCW1    JOB (4887,12),'SORT',
//          CLASS=A,
//          NOTIFY=PBHCW,
//          MSGCLASS=X
//*************************************************
//* SORT A DATA SET
//*************************************************
//SORT05    EXEC PGM=SORT
//SYSIN     DD  *
    SORT FIELDS=(1,20,A),FORMAT=CH
/*
//SORTIN    DD  DSN=data.set.in,
//          DISP=SHR
//SORTWK01 DD  UNIT=SYSDA,        *IF NEEDED
//          SPACE=(CYL,(10,2))
//SORTWK02 DD  UNIT=SYSDA,        *IF NEEDED
//          SPACE=(CYL,(10,2))
//SORTOUT  DD  DSN=sortd.data.set.out,
//          DISP=(NEW,CATLG,DELETE),
//          SPACE=(80,(100,10),RLSE),
//          AVGREC=K,                      *SMS
//          RECFM=FB,LRECL=80,BLKSIZE=0  *ESA
//SYSOUT    DD  SYSOUT=*    *SORT MESSAGES
```

Summary of JCL Updates

8

8.1. NEW WITH ESA V4.1

- Find a brief summary of the new parameters and statements introduced with ESA V4.1 and higher releases of the OS/390 operating system.

- Lists the new parameter, i.e., ADDRESS, then the statement, i.e., OUTPUT where the parameter is coded.

- Also lists new statements such as INCLUDE, JCLLIB, SET.

- ADDRESS-OUTPUT—Aids distribution. It prints on a separator page.

- BUILDING-OUTPUT—Aids distribution. It prints on a separator page.

- COMMAND—Executes JES2 and MVS commands. JES2 only*.

- DEPT-OUTPUT—Aids distribution. It prints on a separator page.

- IF. . .THEN. . .ELSE. . .ENDIF—This statement checks for a valid return code. This newer coding technique can replace COND.

- INCLUDE-DD—Copies a JCL member into a PROC.

  See: JCLLIB statement.

- JCLLIB—Enables PDS(s) to search for INCLUDE and/or PROCLIB member(s).

- NAME-OUTPUT—Aids distribution. It prints on a separator page.

---

* *JES2 4.1/JES3 4.2.1, except COMMAND—any JES2, INCLUDE—any JES2/3.*

- NOTIFY-OUTPUT—Sends print-ended message to a maximum of 4 users.

- OUTDISP-OUTPUT—JES2 only. Controls SYSOUT disposition for normal and abnormal job end.

- ROOM-OUTPUT—Aids distribution. It prints on a separator page.

- SEGMENT-SYSOUT—Starts printing while job is running, even if writing to file. JES2 only*.

- SET—Assigns a value to a symbolic. It can be used to modify PROCs and "Plain JCL."

- SPIN-SYSOUT—Starts printing when the data set is deallocated.

- TIME-EXEC or JOB—NOLIMIT same as 1440, MAXIMUM about 357,912 minutes.

- TITLE-OUTPUT—Aids distribution. It prints on a separator page.

- USERLIB-OUTPUT—Points to libraries that contain Advanced Function Printing (AFP) information (e.g., fonts, page definitions, used by Print Services Facility (PSF), code PAGEDEF OUTPUT parameter to specify the member).

---

* *JES2 4.1/JES3 4.2.1, except SET, SPIN, TIME, USERLIB—any JES2/3.*

8.1.1. Changes with ESA V4.1*

- BLKSIZE-DD—Do not code the BLKSIZE-DD. Let system figure.

- DCB-DD—DCB keyword is not needed.

  See: BLKSIZE, ESA.

- EXEC PROC—Can execute a PROC within a PROC up to 15 levels.

  ☞ Suggest user avoids executing PROC within a PROC.

- LABEL-DD—Is not needed with EXPDT or RETPD.

- ALTER—Changes the limit for number of Generation Data Set(s) (GDSs) in a Generation Data Group (GDG).

ALTER Format
```
ALTER  'dataset.base.name'  LIMIT(##)
```
- Data set concatenation—Allows the following:

1) Can mix tape and DASD.

2) No longer need to code the data set with the largest block size first.

- NULL Statement, ESA—Statement can be used inside the PROC to indicate the end of PROC. (Previously NULL was invalid in a PROC.) NULL can also be used inside an INCLUDE member to indicate the end of member.

  ☞ Caution: If coded in the middle of the PROC, the system stops reading the PROC JCL statements after the //. When NULL is coded in the end of an INCLUDE member, the system continues to read the remaining PROC JCL statements. Valid with JES2.

- PEND—Statement can be coded in PROC.

```
Example:  //            PEND
```

---

* *System must be MVS/ESA with DFP 3.1 or higher.*

- DD Override Order—Statements out of order are not ignored, they are processed—so PROC Overrides can be coded in any order. When adding a new DD to a step, for instance, it had to previously be coded after changes to existing DDs, but now it can be coded before. System will change existing DDs and add the new DD.

- REGION-JOB or EXEC—Region specifies normal (i.e., application address space) and extended (i.e., data space) region size. Range can be 0-9999K. Default for batch jobs is 1M. Coding is 2K-16384K. This storage is allocated below the 16MB line for the application address space, and ESA extended region size defaults to 32M above the 16MB line.

    - Job Output Message IEF374I:

    ...VIRT 96K SYS 220K EXT 4K SYS 9516K

        - Indicates how much virtual storage was used by the job.

        - 96K and 220K are used by the job below the 16MB line.

        - 4K and 9516K are used by the job above the 16MB line.

- Symbolic Names—Up to 8 characters can be used in Symbolic Names. Previously the limit was 7.

- Symbolic Values—Can contain special characters. Don't have to enclose in apostrophes if there is a matching pair of parentheses.

8.2. NEW WITH ESA V4.2

BYTES-JOB—Is the action to take if max output BYTES are exceeded (indicates bytes in thousands).

CARDS-JOB—Is the action to take if max punched CARDS are exceeded (value is 0 - 99999999).

LINES-JOB—Is the action to take if max output LINES are exceeded (indicates lines in thousands).

PAGES-JOB—Is the action to take if max output PAGES are exceeded (value is 0 - 99999999).

&SYSUID*—Symbolic system substitutes the logon id of the person who submitted the job. It is used with APPC/MVS TP Profiles.

---

* *JES2 4.2/JES3 4.2.1, except &SYSUID—JES2 4.1/JES3 4.2.1.*

8.3. NEW SMS PARAMETERS

AVGREC-DD—Requests space in number of records.

  ☞ **See:** *SPACE.*

DATACLAS-DD—Defines data set attributes—e.g.,
 AVGREC/SPACE, KEYLEN-direct data sets, LRECL, RECFM,
 RETPD/EXPDT, vol count of VOLUME—VSAM—CISIZE,
 FREESPACE, IMBED, KEYOFF, RECORG, REPLICATE,
 SHAREOPTIONS.

DSNTYPE-DD—Specifies a Partitioned Data Set Extended
 (PDSE). It must be SMS managed, can have up to 123
 extents, never needs to be compressed, do not specify directory space, has faster access, and can contain load modules.

KEYOFF-DD—Specifies key offset for new VSAM key-sequenced
 data set.

KEYLEN—Specifies length of key in bytes.

LIKE-DD—Copies attributes (e.g., AVGREC, SPACE, DSNTYPE,
 KEYLEN, KEYOFF for VSAM, LRECL, RECFM, RECORG)
 from an existing cataloged data set.

MGMTCLAS-DD—Defines data set attributes for migration and
 backup. It must: limit GDSs on DASD, release unused space,
 archive inactive data sets based on last use, automatically
 restore archived data, and set retention for backed-up versions.

RECORG-DD—Specifies type of VSAM data set being created via
 JCL (e.g., KS, ES, RR, LS).

REFDD-DD—Copies attributes (e.g., AVGREC/SPACE, DSN-
 TYPE, KEYLEN/KEYOFF for VSAM, LRECL, RECFM/
 RECORG for VSAM) from a DD statement. It also copies SMS
 attributes.

SECMODEL-DD—Assigns RACF profile for security and overrides
 and replaces PROTECT.

STORCLAS-DD—Defines data set attributes for service level (performance). This is where SMS stores the data set and controls
 dual copy.

8.3.1. Changes with SMS

SPACE-DD—If coded with AVGREC, the first subparameter means average record length in bytes. For fixed length, use the LRECL.

GDS roll-in states—*Rolled-in* means added to the GDG base at step termination.

&⁄ *See: Appendix F—Job Output SMS Messages #3.*

Bias number (e.g., (+0), (+1)) still does not get updated until the job ends. So just as before, the step must end, then the job must end (even if the job abends in the step following the creation of the GDS).

Deferred roll-in means the GDS was not added to the GDG base. Instead, it was cataloged by G000#V00 number only.

&⁄ *See: Appendix F—Job Output SMS Messages #4.*

☞ Suggest user always code the following disposition when creating a GDS. Never code NEW with KEEP as thic would cause a deferred roll-in.

```
//          DISP=(NEW,CATALOG,DELETE)
```

Example: to roll in a GDS in TSO/ISPF screen 6 key:

```
ALTER    'dataset.G000#V00'   ROLLIN
```

Model DSCB—Is not needed when creating a tape or DASD Generation Data Set (GDS).

&⁄ *See: Standards.*

Before SMS, a model DSCB (i.e., a cataloged data set with no space) had to be coded as the first DCB subparameter when creating a GDS.

&⁄ *See: DCB = model.dataset.*

8.4. VERSION 5 JCL UPDATES

• Covers syntax introduced with this release.

8.4.1. Four-Digit Device Numbers

• With the new Version 5 JCL Updates, there are now 4-digit device numbers, where previously the limit was 3 digits.

• A / must be coded before the 4-digit HEX number.

Example:

```
//          DEST=/####
```

DEST-DD—Can code the 4-digit device—JES3.

Example:

```
//OUT1      DD  SYSOUT=A,DEST=/####
```

UNIT-DD—Coding a device number is not recommended and is ignored if SMS is active.

//*FORMAT PR—Can code the 4-digit device for printed output—JES3.

Example:

```
//*FORMAT  PR  DEST=/A010
```

//*FORMAT PU—Can code the 4-digit device for punched output—JES3.

8.4.2. Version 5 and OpenMVS

DSNTYPE-DD—HFS creates an OpenMVS Hierarchical File System similar to a PDSE. Must code the PATH parameter.

PIPE creates an OpenMVS FIFO file where data is read on a first-in, first-out basis. Must code the PATH parameter instead of the DSN.

Example HFS

```
//          DSNTYPE=HFS
```

Example PIPE

```
//          DSNTYPE=PIPE
```

PATH-DD—gives the HFS directory names from the root to the file name. The name can be up to 254 characters, is case-sensitive, and must be enclosed in apostrophes. If not in apostrophes, it must be in uppercase, numbers, $ sign, @ sign, # sign, /, *, +, -, or a period.

Example:

```
//IN1      DD  PATH='openmvs/acctng/janfile'
```

PATHDISP-DD—KEEP or DELETE specifies what to do with HFS file if step ends normally and if the step abends.

Example:

```
//          PATHDISP=(KEEP,KEEP)
```

PATHMODE-DD—Must be coded when creating a file or no users can access the file. If file exists, PATHMODE is syntax checked and ignored.

- SIRUSR—Owner can read file.

- SIWUSR—Owner can write file.

- SIXUSR—Owner can search directory or execute a program.

- SIRWXU—Owner can read, write, search, or execute.

- SIRGRP—Group can read file.

- SIWGRP—Group can write file.

- SIXGRP—Group can search directory or execute a program.

- SIRWXG—Group can read, write, search, or execute.

- SIROTH—Other can read file.

- SIWOTH—Other can write file.

- SIXOTH—Other can search directory or execute a program.

- SIRWXO—Other can read, write, search, or execute.

Examples:

```
//          PATHMODE=(SIRUSR,SIWUSR,SIXUSR)
               or
//          PATHMODE=SIRWXU
```

PATHOPTS-DD—System uses PATHOPTS to get the file status. File is NEW if PATHOPTS contains OCREAT and OEXCL, MOD. If PATHOPTS contains OCREAT without OEXCL, file is OLD. The two types are access group and status group. Up to 7 options can be coded, in any order. Code only 1 access group option or system uses ORDWR.

- Access Group:

  1) ORDONLY—Access group is read.

  2) OWRONLY—Access group is write.

  3) ORDWR—Access group is read, write; do not code for FIFO files.

- Status Group:

  1) OAPPEND—Write data at the end of the file.

  2) OCREAT—Create file, not a directory. All directories must exist or file will not be created.

  See: OEXCL, below.

  3) OEXCL—Create file if it does not exist. Abend job step if file exists. Parameter is ignored if OCREAT is not coded.

  4) ONOCTTY—If PATH specifies a terminal device, opening the file does not make that terminal the controlling terminal for the process.

  5) ONONBLOCK and ORDONLY—FIFO special file-open for read-only returns without delay. Without ORDONLY, an open for read-only waits until a process opens the file for writing.

  6) ONONBLOCK and OWRONLY—FIFO special file-open for write-only gives an error if file is not already open for reading. Without OWRONLY, an open for write-only waits until the file is opened for reading.

  7) ONONBLOCK—Character special file with non-blocking open-open returns without waiting until the device is ready, else the open waits until the device is ready.

8) OSYNC—Move data from the buffer to permanent storage before returning control from a callable service.

9) OTRUNC—Truncate the file to 0 if the file exists, is a regular file, or was opened with ORDWR or OWRONLY.

Example:
```
//           PATHOPTS=(ORDWR,OCREAT)
```
***EXAMPLE** Create a File*
```
//OUT1     DD  PATH='/openmvs/acctng/janfile',
//             DSNTYPE=PIPE,PATHOPTS=(OWRONLY,OCREAT),
//             PATHDISP=(KEEP,DELETE),PATHMODE=SIWGRP
```

- A concatenated HFS file cannot be written or read; yet the concatenation does not result in a JCL error.

8.4.3. Started Tasks with JOB Statements

User can assign accounting information, pass a PARM, and control printed output for started tasks with the JOB statement. Currently, started tasks are procedures and the system adds a JOB and EXEC statement when the procedure is started.

Example
```
//INIT     JOB (accounting),'INITIATORS',
//             MSGLEVEL=1
//JESDS    OUTPUT JESDS=ALL,
//             OUTDISP=(PURGE,WRITE)
//JS001    EXEC PROC=INIT
//
```

Appendixes

APPENDIX A

Acronyms

ABEND	ABnormal END
ACS	Automatic Class Selection
AFP	Advanced Function Printing
APPC	Advanced Program-to-Program Communication
BPI	Bits Per Inch
COBOL	COmmon Business Oriented Language
DASD	Direct Access Storage Device
DCB	Data Control Block
DD	Data Definition
DFDSS	Data Facility Data Set Services
DFHSM	Data Facility Hierarchical Storage Manager
DFP	Data Facility Product
DFSMS	Data Facility Storage Management Subsystem (or SMS)
DSN	Data Set Name
ESA	Enterprise Systems Architecture
ESDS	Entry Sequenced Data Set (VSAM)
FIFO	First-In-First-Out File (OpenMVS)
GDG	Generation Data Group
GDS	Generation Data Set
HFS	Hierarchical File System (OpenMVS)

IBM	International Business Machines Corporation
IMS	Information Management System
I/O	Input/Output
ISMF	Interactive Storage Management Facility
ISPF	Interactive System Productivity Facility (TSO)
JCL	Job Control Language
JES	Job Entry Subsystem
KSDS	Key Sequenced Data Set (VSAM)
LSDS	Linear Space Data Set (VSAM)
MVS	Multiple Virtual Storage
MVS/ESA	Multiple Virtual Storage/Enterprise Systems Architecture
MVS/SP	Multiple Virtual Storage/System Product
MVS/XA	Multiple Virtual Storage/eXtended Architecture
OS/390	Operating System 390 (new name for MVS/ESA version 5 and higher)
PDS	Partitioned Data Set
PDSE	Partitioned Data Set Extended
PROC	PROCedure
PSF	Print Services Facility
RACF	Resource Access Control Facility
RC	Return Code *(also called completion code and COND CODE)*
RDS	Retention Data Set (CA-1)
RRDS	Relative Record Data Set (VSAM)
SMS	Storage Management Subsystem or System Managed Storage
STC	Started Task
TP	Transaction Program (APPC)
TSO	Time Sharing Option
VSAM	Virtual Storage Access Method

APPENDIX B

JES2 PROC Example

```
//JES2       PROC
//** ** ** ** ** ** ** ** ** ** ** ** ** **
//*  JES2 SUSBYSTEM
//** ** ** ** ** ** ** ** ** ** ** ** ** **
//IEFPROC  EXEC PGM=HASJES20,DPRTY=(15,15),
//              TIME=1440,
//              PERFORM=9
//PROC00   DD   DSN=SYS1.PROCLIB,
//              DISP=SHR
//         DD   DSN=PROD.LIB.PROCLIB,
//              DISP=SHR
//PROC01   DD   DSN=TEST.LIB.PROCLIB,
//              DISP=SHR
//PROC02   DD   DSN=PAYTST.LIB.PROCLIB,
//              DISP=SHR
```

Older Coding:

- PROCLIB(s) had to be defined in the JES2 PROC. When PROCLIB(s) are defined as part of the PROC00 DD statement the system automatically searches the PROCLIB libraries in the order coded. First, SYS1.PROCLIB, then PROD.LIB.PROCLIB.

- If the system doesn't find the PROC in the libraries, job gets a JCL error: "PROCEDURE NOT FOUND."

- If user wants to search a library not defined on the PROC00 DD statement such as TEST.LIB.PROCLIB, you must code a JES JCL statement telling system what library you want to search:

  ```
  /* JOBPARM PROCLIB=PROC01
  ```

- Or your Systems Programmer can set up your system to search libraries based on what you code in the job statement CLASS parameter. See your JCL standards.

- MVS/ESA introduces the JCLLIB statement; PROCLIBs no longer need to be defined to the JES PROC.

  ☞ Suggest user code the JCLLIB statement instead of the /*JOBPARM as JCLLIB is a better method.

APPENDIX C

JES2 Job CLASS Display

* When the command is performed through ISPF SDSF user must precede the command with a /.

* There are many defaults built into the class such as a region size, time, also where the system should look for the PROC.

* PROCLIB=00 tells system to search the libraries concatenated on the PROC00 DD in the JES2 PROC. See Appendix A.

JES2 Command Example

```
$DJOBCLASS(A)
```

System Displays

HASP837 JOBCLASS(A)

```
HASP837    ACCT=YES,PGMRNAME=YES,TIME=(000030,
HASP837    00),REGION=4096K,COMMAND=IGNORE,
HASP837    BLP=NO,AUTH=(INFO),MSGLEVEL=(1,1),
HASP837    COPY=NO,HOLD=NO,IEFUJP=YES,
HASP837    IEFUSO=YES,JOURNAL=NO,LOG=YES,
HASP837    MODE=JES,OUTDISP=(,),OUTPUT=YES,
HASP837    PERFORM=000,PROCLIB=00,QHELD=NO,
HASP837    RESTART=NO,SCAN=NO,SCHENV=,
HASP837    SWA=BELOW,TYPE26=YES,TYPE6=YES,
HASP837    XBM=,XEQCOUNT=(MAXIMUM=*,CURRENT=0)
```

APPENDIX D

Job Output and Return Codes

* JOBNAME is found in columns 3–10 on job statement.
* STEPNAME is found in columns 3–10 on EXEC PROC statement.
* PROCSTEP is found in columns 3–10 on EXEC PGM.
* RC indicates return code or completion code whether the program ran successfully.

If there is a problem with the job, review these messages. The messages indicate where the problem is.

"Plain JCL" Top of JES2 Job Log Summary Example:

```
JOB05722   -JOBNAME   STEPNAME PROCSTEP   RC
JOB05722   -PROD4              BR1405     00
JOB05722   -PROD4              BACK05     08
```

"Plain JCL" Message for Each Step Format:

```
IEF142I jobname stepname-STEP WAS EXECUTED-COND CODE nnnn
```

"Plain JCL" Message for Each Step Example:

```
IEF142I PROD4 BACK05-STEP WAS EXECUTED-COND CODE 0008
```

"PROC" Top of JES2 Job Log Summary Example:

```
JOB05722   -JOBNAME   STEPNAME PROCSTEP   RC
JOB05722   -PAYD001   JS001    UPDT05     00
JOB05722   -PAYD001   JS001    REPT05     00
```

"PROC" Message for Each Step Format:

```
IEF142I jobname procstep jobstep-STEP WAS EXECUTED-COND CODE nnnn
```

"PROC" Message for Each Step Example:

```
IEF142I PAYD001 UPDT05 JS001-STEP WAS EXECUTED-COND CODE 0000
```

APPENDIX D

Job Output and Return Codes (Continued)

• Find a list of return or condition codes and their meanings per IBM standards.

RC	Meaning
0000	No errors or warnings detected. Run is successful.
0004	Might be warnings. Run should be successful.
0008	Serious errors. Run was not successful.
0012	Serious errors. Run was not successful.
0016	Terminal error. Run was not successful.
0020	Terminal error. Run was not successful.

APPENDIX E

Job ABEND Output Example

```
JOB01508 ---- Monday,   09 JUL 2000 ----
JOB01508 IRR010I  USERID BRITT I  IS ASSIGNED TO THIS JOB.
JOB01508 $HASP373 BRITT4  - STARTED - INIT 9  - CLASS 4 SYS SYSA
JOB01508 IEF403I  BRITT4  - STARTED - TIME=16.10.42
JOB01508 IEW4000I FETCH FOR MODULE IDCAMS   FROM DDNAME -LNKLST-
JOB01508 CSV031I  LIBRARY ACCESS FAILED FOR MODULE IDCAMS , RETURN…
JOB01508 CSV028I  ABEND106-28 JOBNAME=BRITT4   STEPNAME=STEP01
JOB01508 IEA995I  SYMPTOM DUMP OUTPUT
                  SYSTEM COMPLETION CODE=106   REASON CODE=00000028
                  TIME=16.10.42  SEQ=44355  CPU=0000  ASID=0058
                  PSW AT TIME OF ERROR  070C1000   811E2AA2 …
                  NO ACTIVE MODULE FOUND …
                  GPR  0-3…
JOB01508 IEF450I  BRITT4  STEP01 - ABEND-106 U0000 REASON=00000028
JOB01508 JOBNAME STEPNAME PROCSTEP    RC
JOB01508 BRITT4             STEP01  *S106  …
JOB01508 BRITT4             STEP05  FLUSH  …
```

- IEW4000I—First message that indicates there is a problem. First 3 letters of a message give the OS/390 subsystem or 3rd party software that issued the message. An "I" at end of message indicates message is informational.

- CSV031I—Second message that indicates there is a problem.

- CSV028I—Third that indicates there is a problem. All job messages can be looked up; the best message to look up for help with above error is the system completion and reason code. *Look up the error message* instead of guessing the reason for the abend.

- SYSTEM COMPLETION CODE **106***—Means there was not enough storage available to load program module IDCAMS. Can also be researched in IBM System Codes manual.

- REASON CODE **28**—Gives further information about the error. Look up correct reason code when researching the ABEND.

- Shows the job abended in STEP01. When a job abends, the rest of the steps FLUSH (do not run).

- Corrective action—REGION parameter must be added or increased.

---

* *MVS/Quick-Ref has JCL syntax available on-line, and user can place their cursor on an error message, hit a PF Key, and the product displays the error message. Best placement of the cursor is on this message.*

APPENDIX F

Job Output SMS Messages (IGD)

1) Following message displays for a DASD data set when it's being created. (Remember, all SMS managed data sets are cataloged.)

```
IGD101I  SMS ALLOCATED TO DDNAME (DD01    )
   DSN  (dataset.name                      )
STORCLAS    (TRAN1) MGMTCLAS(TRAN1) DATACLAS (  )
```

2) Following message displays for a DASD data set when it's being kept.

```
IGD104I  dataset.name      RETAINED, DDNAME=SYSUT1
```

3) Except for GDS DASD data sets, this message appears instead of above message. It means the data set was cataloged and rolled into the GDG (can access using the bias number (+0)):

```
IGD107I  dataset.G000#V00  ROLLED IN, DDNAME=SYSUT2
```

4) This means that the GDS DASD data set was cataloged by G000#V00, but not rolled into the GDG (cannot access using the bias number (+0)):

```
IGD104I  dataset.G000#V00 RETAINED, DDNAME=SYSUT2
```

5) This means that the GDS tape data set was cataloged (can access using the bias number (+0)):

```
IEF285I  dataset.G000#V00      CATALOGED
```

APPENDIX G

Job Output JCL Columns 1 and 2

The following characters print in columns 1 and 2 of the job output:

Columns

1- 2	Meaning
/ /	JCL from JCLLIB or "Plain JCL".
xx	PROC statement from PROCLIB.
/ /	JCL from JCLLIB. For DD overrides MVS uses this statement. This statement is found before the next statement X/ indicating a PROC statement being overridden.
x/	PROC statement, changed using an override.
/ /*	JCLLIB or the little PDS comment statement.
xx*	Means a PROC comment statement.
++	Means an in-stream procedure statement.
+/	In-stream PROC statement changed using an override.
++*	Means an in-stream procedure comment statement.
***	JES2 or JES3 statement.

APPENDIX H

How to Pass a Return Code from a Program

* Whenever processing must stop, pass a return code from the program and call the shop's ABEND routine. To issue a return code from a program use a number from 0-4095.

* VS COBOL II generates user abends of U1000 to U1999. Try to avoid using these codes.

* LE/370 generates user abends: U4000 to U4095. Try to avoid using these codes.

Assembler:	`Put rc in general register 15.`
C:	`exit(rc).`
COBOL Format:	`MOVE rc TO RETURN-CODE.`
COBOL Example:	`MOVE 99 TO RETURN-CODE.`
FORTRAN:	`STOP rc.`
PL/I:	`CALL PLIRETC(rc).`

APPENDIX I

DASD Capacity

3380 AD4, BD4, AJ4, BJ4

47,476 bytes/track, 15 TRKS/CYL, 885 CYLs/volume - 630 MB.

• Average seek time in milliseconds: 15.

• Average rotational delay in milliseconds: 8.3.

3380 AE4, BE4

47,476 bytes/track, 15 TRKS/CYL, 1770 CYLs/volume-1260 MB.

• Average seek time in milliseconds: 17.

• Average rotational delay in milliseconds: 8.3.

3380 AK4, BK4

47,476 bytes/track, 15 TRKS/CYL, 2655 CYLs/volume -1890 MB.

• Average seek time in milliseconds: 15.

• Average rotational delay in milliseconds: 8.3.

3390 A14, B14, A18, B18, B1C

56,664 bytes/track, 15 TRKS/CYL, 1113 CYLs/volume - 946 MB.

• Average seek time in milliseconds: 9.5.

• Average rotational delay in milliseconds: 7.1.

3390 A24, B24, A38, B28, B2C

56,664 bytes/track, 15 TRKS/CYL, 2226 CYLs/volume -1892 MB.

• Average seek time in milliseconds: 12.5.

• Average rotational delay in milliseconds: 7.1.

• If user is still figuring the block size for DASD data sets the user must know the bytes per track.*

• If user is not asking for space using AVGREC then bytes per track is also used to calculate space. User figures number of records that fit in a block and number of blocks that fit in a track to calculate appropriate space.

---

* *When operating system is not MVS/ESA 4.1 or a higher release such as OS/390.*

What did you think of this book?

Subject: Getting your input on the
OS/390 MVS JCL Quick Reference Guide

Dear Reader,

Please let me know what you think about our OS/390 MVS JCL Quick Reference Guide. What did you especially like?

What do you think needs more in-depth explanation? Were there any errors? And so on.

Are there any topical areas or issues that you'd like us to address in our series?

E-mail me with your comments at ocarmandi@mvs-training.com or write to me at 600 Commerce Drive, Suite 605, Pittsburgh, PA 15108. Please include:

Your Name, Company, Address, Phone, E-mail

We look forward to receiving your input on this book and the series. Thank you for helping to improve the series.

Best Regards,

Olivia R. Carmandi

Olivia R. Carmandi

P.S. If you have a specific JCL question fell free to call or e-mail me.

Index